By the Editors of Consumer Guide®

Pressure
Cooker Cookbook

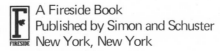
A Fireside Book
Published by Simon and Schuster
New York, New York

Contents

Contents

Contents

Louis Weber, President
Publications International, Ltd.
3841 West Oakton Street
Skokie, Illinois 60076

Permission is never granted for commercial purposes

Manufactured in the United States of America
1 2 3 4 5 6 7 8 9 10

A Fireside Book
Published by Simon & Schuster
A Division of Gulf + Western Corporation
New York, New York 10020
Library of Congress Cataloging
in Publication Data
Main Entry under title:
Pressure cooker cookbook.
    (A Fireside book)
    Includes index.
    1. Pressure cookery.   I. Consumer guide.
TX840.P7P72   641.5'87   78-15471
ISBN 0-671-24386-1 pbk.
Illustrations By: Nan Brooks
Cover Design: Frank E. Peiler
Photography By: Dave Jordano

Introduction

PRESSURE COOKING has come a long way since the cooker was invented 300 years ago. Today, it's not only the fastest way to cook, but also the most reliable. It offers not only one-pot convenience, but also remarkable versatility—making it possible to prepare everything from hearty homemade soups to elegant entrées to succulent vegetables, fluffy custards, steamed puddings and even complete three-course dinners in a matter of minutes.

Changes in pressure cooker design have made recent models incomparably easier and safer to use than the older units. The new models feature cover locks that make it difficult, if not impossible, to open the cooker before pressure has been reduced. So the old fear of food spattering up in a geyser of steam when the cooker is opened has been eliminated — it can't happen once pressure has been reduced. Another old-fashioned problem that also has been eliminated is that of maintaining the proper pressure level; the automatic pressure regulators now available on almost all models ensure that the desired pressure level will remain constant. You can maintain complete control over the cooking process and count on successful results every time.

Electric pressure cookers, like Presto's Gran-Cookerie and WeeCookerie, offer dramatically updated cooking convenience. Not only are they portable, allowing you to prepare whole meals at the table, but with these cookers you never have to worry about adjusting the heat under the pot — the electric heat regulators, similar to those on electric fry pans, are virtually foolproof.

Perhaps the most significant new development has been the introduction of low-pressure fryers, both stovetop and electric, by Wear-Ever and Presto. These fryers are truly a sign of the times: They offer both the speed of regular pressure cooking and the singular opportunity to make "Kentucky-fried"-type chicken at home that's much fresher and tastier than the Colonel's. You can use them as well to deep-fry irresistible onion rings, mushrooms and other vegetables, crispy fish fillets, fruit fritters and more.

Improvements in pressure cookers make meal preparation much easier on the cook, but good eating remains at the heart of the matter. Because you can steam foods faster and at higher temperatures than conventional methods allow, you often can create more tantalizing flavor blends and achieve better food texture in the pressure cooker than you can any other way. The recipes in this book take advantage of this potential. You will find delicious combinations of ingredients and seasonings in every chapter — from stocks and soups through main courses and vegetables to desserts, steamed breads and puddings, pressure canning and low-pressure frying.

In the full-color "Techniques" and "Recipe How-to's" sections, you'll find step-by-step illustrations of the best methods to use for all kinds of pressure cookery. Refer to these, as well as the following discussion of techniques, and you'll become well-acquainted with the mealtime pleasure and convenience your cooker can provide. For detailed descriptions and evaluations of various pressure cooker models, turn to our "Test Reports" on page 153.

What Is Pressure Cooking?

Pressure cooking is simply a matter of heating water or other liquid to temperatures higher than those that can be attained under normal atmospheric conditions and then cooking foods in the super-heated steam. Normal air pressure at sea level is 14.7 pounds per-square-inch; at this pressure, boiling water attains a temperature of 212°F (100°C). You cannot raise the temperature at which water boils unless you raise the level of pressure around it. But if you increase pressure by 5 pounds per-square-inch, you can raise the temperature of the boiling liquid and its steam to 228°F (109°C). Raise it by 10 pounds per-square-inch and the water will boil at 238°F (114°C); with 15 pounds per-square-inch of additional pressure, the temperature of the boiling liquid and steam will be 250°F (121°C). (At high altitudes the temperatures will be lower because normal air pressure is lower than 14.7 pounds per-square-inch; so cooking times at 15 pounds of additional pressure have to be increased by 5% for every 1000 feet above 2000 feet to compensate for the lower temperature.)

How is the pressure increased? By trapping the steam created when water boils in a tightly enclosed space. The process can be discussed in far greater detail, but these are the basic facts you need to understand cooker techniques.

It follows that the two things essential to pressure cooking are water, or another liquid, and a strong, tightly-sealed pot. You also, of course, need to be able to heat the water in the pot to create steam. And, equally importantly, you have to be able to tell how much steam is being trapped in the pot so that you know at what pressure level the water is boiling, and, consequently, what temperature is being maintained. For cooking purposes, you would not want to lock in all of the steam created as the liquid boils because the pressure and the temperature would rise to the point where food would cook too quickly to preserve flavor and texture. You want to be able to take advantage of the speed of high-temperature pressure cooking without losing control over the quality of the finished food.

Choosing A Cooker

Because all pressure cookers work on the same principle, there are few fundamental differences among them. All cookers must close tightly enough so that steam cannot escape between the pot and the lid; most achieve this seal with a rubber gasket but at least one model does so with a half dozen lid clamps. All cookers must have some type of vent through which excess steam can escape. All cookers must have some way of letting you know if there is steam pressure inside the pot and almost all cookers have some device for letting you know how much pressure — and, thus, what temperature — has been reached. On some cookers, there is a dial separate from the steam vent that indicates pressure level; most cookers come with a regulator that fits over the steam vent and automatically maintains pressure at a given level — usually 15 pounds.

Many people prefer the versatility of cookers

that can be regulated at either 5, 10 or 15 pounds of pressure, either because they claim that the lower pressure levels produce better texture in some foods or because they do a lot of home canning, which usually calls for 5 or 10 pounds of pressure. All you really need for everyday pressure cooking, however, is a cooker that will maintain 15 pounds of pressure. (For further discussion of various models, see Test Reports, page 153.)

One recent development in pressure cooker design does offer a significant convenience, especially to owners of electric ranges. Most pressure cookers are stovetop models and, like any other stovetop pots and pans, they require some judgment on the part of the cook as to the heat level needed to maintain proper cooking temperature, although automatic pressure regulators do remove much of the guesswork. But the new electric cookers, made by Presto, allow you to set a heat regulator to the proper temperature; there's no room for error because all you have to do, once pressure has been reached, is turn down the dial until the pilot light goes out. With a gas range, you can accomplish much the same effect by lowering the flame, but with an electric range, you have to remove the cooker from the burner for a minute or two in order to reduce the heat. So owners of electric ranges may well appreciate the convenience offered by the electric cookers.

You will find that virtually every pressure cooker model on the market comes in more than one size. Because steam will expand to fill any size cooker and will cook all food in the cooker at the same rate, the size of the cooker you choose will not affect the minimum amount of food you can cook in it. It definitely will affect the maximum amount of food you can fit in it — you should never fill any cooker more than two-thirds or three-fourths full, according to the manufacturer's directions. And it will affect the amount of water you must use to fill the cooker with steam.

Like any other cooking method, pressure cooking has certain dangers. If you understand the principles of pressure cooking, you can anticipate the hazards:

1) If there is no water or other liquid in the pot, there can't be any steam; so food left to cook without sufficient water will burn.

2) If you leave a cooker on heat set higher than is necessary to maintain pressure, you'll

create too much steam too quickly to cook effectively.

3) If the vent that allows steam to escape from the pot becomes blocked or clogged with food (and if you overfill the cooker, you are increasing this danger), the steam pressure will continue to increase beyond the point at which it can be controlled for cooking purposes.

You can easily avoid these dangers with these precautions:

1) Always use at least the amount of water or other liquid specified in a recipe (and increase that amount as directed by the manufacturer for cookers larger than 8 quarts).

2) Always turn down the heat under your pressure cooker once pressure has been reached. Follow the manufacturer's directions for maintaining the pressure level you want — whether it's signified by "one to four jiggles per minute" or "gently rocking" or a dial number.

3) Always check that the vent tube is clear by holding the lid up to the light before you close your cooker. Light should be visible; if it isn't, clear the tube by inserting a wire or a pipe cleaner to remove whatever is blocking it. To help prevent the vent tube from becoming clogged, avoid pressure cooking those foods such as applesauce, pearl barley, split peas, cranberries and rhubarb, that tend to foam and froth. If the vent should become clogged during cooking, or if the cooking liquid should boil away, there is a safety valve of some kind built into every cooker; this valve will "blow off" to release the pressure. You will have to replace the valve before you can use the cooker again.

One last precaution will ensure safe pressure cooking: Never try to open a cooker while there's steam pressure inside. And never open a cooker without first lifting the pressure regulator to check for steam. Obviously, the same super-heated steam that cooks food so quickly can also produce a terrible burn.

Using The Cooker You Choose

Read the instruction manual that comes with your cooker. Carefully note directions for assembling and cleaning the cooker; these will differ from model to model.

Before you try any recipes, give the cooker a trial run: Pour two cups of water into the pot. Check the vent tube by holding the cover up to the light; light should be visible through it.

Close the lid according to manufacturer's directions. Put the pressure regulator in place; set it for 15 pounds pressure if you have more than one setting. Heat the pot over high heat until pressure is reached. Reduce the heat until the regulator (or pressure dial) indicates, according to manufacturer's instructions, that pressure is being maintained. "Cook" the water for 10 minutes; get used to setting a minute timer for the cooking time required — you will need to use the timer with all pressure cooker recipes. Then turn off the heat and remove the pot from the burner. Let the cooker cool until all pressure has been reduced. It will take about three to five minutes for the pressure to be reduced. (The longer the cooking time, the longer it takes for pressure to be reduced naturally.) After three minutes, lift the regulator slightly and check to see if steam comes out. If steam comes out of the vent tube, allow the cooker to cool a few more minutes. If there is no steam, lift off the regulator and open the cooker.

The first trial run should acquaint you with how to close your cooker correctly, how to tell when pressure is reached, how to maintain pressure with low heat, and how to check for pressure reduction. It's very important not only that you master these techniques before you start cooking, but also that you feel comfortable using the cooker. So go through another trial run: Start with cold water in the cooker, check the vent tube, close the cooker, put the regulator in place, bring the cooker to pressure and maintain pressure for ten minutes. But this time, do not wait for pressure to be reduced naturally. Instead, turn off the heat and lift the pressure cooker into the sink. Let cold water run over the lid of the cooker for about thirty seconds. Then lift the pressure regulator slightly and check for steam. If steam comes out, continue running the cold water another minute or so. Lift the regulator slightly and check again; if no steam comes out, remove the regulator and open the cooker. This is the method of pressure reduction you will use whenever a recipe calls for you to reduce pressure immediately. An alternative to this method is to place the cooker in a pan of cool water rather than under the faucet in the sink.

You will notice when you begin to cook that some recipes call for you to reduce pressure naturally. Others specify that you reduce pressure immediately by placing the cooker under cold, running water. Still others require that you reduce pressure naturally for five minutes and then complete pressure reduction by placing the cooker under cold, running water. The distinction is based on the type of food being cooked; the texture of some foods will be adversely affected if you reduce the pressure too quickly — for example, beans and lentils might pop open and meat fibers might separate. Follow the specific recipe directions for reducing pressure. And always reduce pressure naturally where you are using the cooker for canning.

Cooking At Pressure

The first thing you'll notice about pressure cooker recipes is that they call for relatively short cooking times — some only a few minutes. Indeed, some recipes say "Cook 0 minutes," which means that you should bring the cooker to the pressure level specified and then begin to reduce pressure as directed. There is no cooking under pressure; the amount of heat required to bring the cooker to pressure is sufficient to cook the food. Usually, however, some cooking under pressure is required and you'll need a minute timer in order to follow the recipes correctly. Timing is often critical in pressure cooking because the temperature inside the cooker is so high.

Because timing is so important, you should be aware of the factors that affect it in various recipes. One factor, of course, is the pressure level: Since at 15 pounds pressure you are cooking at 250°F (121°C), while at 5 pounds pressure the temperature is 228°F (109°C), foods will cook faster at 15 pounds pressure.

Another time criterion is how well done you want the food to be. With some recipes, such as those for custards and puddings, there is little or no time allowance for judgments of taste: The food is either done or not done. But especially with meats, poultry, fish and vegetables, there is room for cooking discretion based on taste and you can easily learn to adjust recipes accordingly. If you like meat rare, poultry chewy and vegetables crisp, for example, then cook fewer minutes than the recipe specifies. To test for doneness, reduce pressure according to the recipe, open the cooker, and pierce the food with a fork or slice off a small piece. If the

food is underdone, you can always put it back in the cooker, bring the cooker back up to pressure and cook the food a little longer. You can follow the same procedure if even the full amount of time given in a recipe is less than you would like. The only precaution you need take is to make sure there is enough liquid left in the cooker to return it to pressure. After a few tries, you will develop a sense of timing adjusted to your own taste.

There are several other factors that affect timing and you can learn to use these to cook foods faster or more slowly. Size of the foods to be cooked will affect cooking times: A potato cut into $1/4$ inch slices, for example, will cook in about one-fifth of the time required to cook a whole potato. An inch-thick bottom round steak will cook in less than 15 minutes, while a bottom round roast takes about an hour. So the rule of thumb is: If you want food to cook more quickly, cut it into smaller pieces. This also means, however, that if you are using pieces of meat, fish, poultry, vegetables or fruits smaller or larger than those specified in a recipe, you should adjust cooking times accordingly.

Sometimes it is desirable to slow down the cooking process for foods of a given size or volume — either to coordinate the cooking of two foods, such as a pork chop and a sliced potato, that require different times or to improve the texture of a food such as a pot roast or a custard. One way to do this is to wrap foods in aluminum foil. Another way is to steam them in glass or ceramic containers tightly covered with foil.

Almost every pressure cooker comes with a cooking rack and this device is so handy that you may want to order a second one from the manufacturer, although a round wire cake cooling rack can serve the same purpose. When do you use the rack? Most importantly, whenever you're steaming foods such as casseroles, custards or breads in bowls, molds and other containers, as well as for pressure canning. Additionally, whenever you want foods — such as roasts, chops, or vegetables — to cook in steam rather than directly in boiling liquid.

If you're cooking several foods and you don't want flavors to mingle, use the rack, because the steam won't cause food aromas to blend as boiling liquid will. You can also use the rack to separate layers of food or to stack tiers of custard cups or casseroles — always being certain not to fill the cooker more than two-thirds or three-fourths full, according to manufacturer's directions.

One of the greatest conveniences of pressure cooking is the versatility of the pot itself. Aside from the fact that you can pressure steam several foods in it at once, the cooker also features the advantages of sturdy construction and even heat conduction for browning meats and poultry and for simmering sauces. Many pressure cooker recipes call for three- and even four-stage cooking in the single pot.

Low-Pressure Frying

The appearance of specially-designed low-pressure fryers on the market heralds an exciting new development in pressure cooking. The low-pressure fryers, currently made by Wear-Ever and Presto, operate at 5 pounds pressure and can be used with water or other liquid like standard pressure cookers. But they also have special vents that allow you to use them with vegetable oil instead of water. So you can pressure deep-fry in them as well as pressure steam. The low-pressure fryers produce uniquely delicious fried foods that feature the crispness of deep frying as well as the moistness of regular pressure cooking. You cannot prepare low-pressure fried foods in a standard cooker and you should never attempt to do so.

The low-pressure fryers require cooking techniques somewhat different from those used with standard cookers. When you are using them for deep frying, you first heat the amount of vegetable oil specified to the temperature given in the recipe. Then you add the foods to be fried and, usually but not always, brown them in the oil with the fryer uncovered. After this step, the foods are covered and cooked at 5 pounds of pressure and the pressure regulator should jiggle or rock at a gentle pace, according to manufacturer's directions, while the cooker is under pressure. But please note that the actual low-pressure frying time is measured from the moment that the cover is securely fastened — not from the time when pressure is reached. When low-pressure frying has been completed, you reduce pressure by lifting the regulator — without removing it — and letting the steam escape. The methods used for reducing pressure in standard cookers should never be used when you are low-pressure frying with vegetable oil. For a more detailed discussion of low-pressure frying, see page 137.

METRIC EQUIVALENTS FOR PRESSURE COOKER RECIPES

INGREDIENTS:

Measure	Equivalent	Metric
1/4 tsp		1 mL
1/2 tsp		2 mL
1 tsp		5 mL
1 Tbsp	3 tsp	15 mL
2 Tbsp	1 fl oz	30 mL
1/4 c		60 mL
1/3 c	5 Tbsp + 1 tsp	80 mL
1/2 c	8 Tbsp	125 mL
1 c	16 Tbsp	250 mL
1 pt	2 c	500 mL
1 qt	4 c	1 L
1 oz (dry)	2 Tbsp	30 g
1 lb	16 oz	450 g
2. 21 lb	35.3 oz	1 kg

mL: milliliter; L: liter; g: gram; kg: kilogram; fl oz: fluid ounces; c: cup

BOWLS AND CASSEROLES:

Size	Metric Volume
1 qt	1 L
1 1/2 qt	1.5 L
2 qt	2 L

OVEN SETTING

°Fahrenheit	°Celsius
250	120
300	150
325	160
350	180
400	200
425	220
450	230
475	250

LOW-PRESSURE FRYING TEMPERATURES

°Fahrenheit	°Celsius
350	175
375	190

DIMENSIONS

Measure	Metric	Equivalent
1 in	25 mm	2.5 cm
1 1/2 in	40 mm	4 cm
2 in	5 cm	
2 1/2 in	6 cm	
3 in	8 cm	
4 in	10 cm	

in: inches; mm: millimeters; cm: centimeters

Techniques

Pressure cookers are truly easy to use once you've mastered the simple techniques. Every model is slightly different; so it is very important that you read the instruction manual for your cooker. But the same basic cooking methods apply for all models.

Cooker Features

Mirro Deluxe

Like the Mirro-Matic Deluxe model, most cookers come with a rack used to keep foods above the cooking liquid, to steam food in containers or to separate two layers of food.

To achieve pressure, you must close the cooker securely. Position the Mirro cover so that you can rotate the cover handle.

Techniques

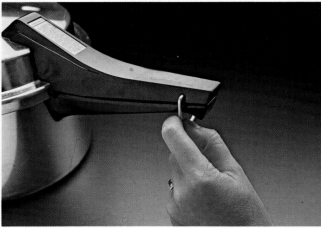

Rotate the cover clockwise until the cover handle is directly over the pot handle.

The reminder ring should drop easily over the pot handle, indicating that the cooker is properly closed.

You can cook at either 5, 10, or 15 pounds of pressure with the Mirro Deluxe by positioning the regulator accordingly on the vent tube.

Presto Electric

To ensure proper closing, the cover on Presto's electric cooker will only fit on the pot in one position and rotate closed in one direction.

The Presto pressure regulator maintains a steady pressure of 15 pounds. It rocks back and forth when pressure is reached.

Techniques

Plug the Presto Control Master heat control into the cooker and set it at 400°F until pressure is reached; then turn the heat down until the pilot light goes out to maintain 15 pounds of pressure. Timing begins when the heat is turned down.

SEB

The clamp must be tight against the lid before you can slide the lid of the SEB cooker onto the pot and fit it into the rim.

To lock the lid into position, you tighten the knob by turning it twice in the direction of the arrow.

Place the rotating pressure regulator on the SEB vent pipe and it will maintain pressure at 8 pounds.

11

All-American

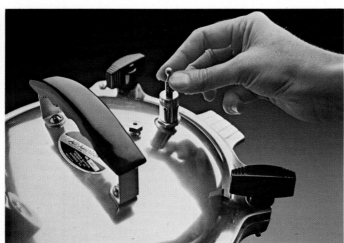

The lids of the All-American cookers have a gauge that indicates pressure level. You regulate pressure by controlling the heat under the pot.

To close the cooker, place the cover on the pot. Then grasp any two opposite knobs and tighten them at the same time. Continue until all are fastened.

Leave the control valve upright in the open position until steam escapes freely; then turn it to a horizontal position to maintain pressure.

Cover Lock

Many cookers have a cover lock that prevents them from being opened while there is pressure inside. When the Presto cooker is properly closed and pressure begins to build, the air vent/cover lock near the edge of the cover rises and locks the cooker shut. When pressure is reduced, the air vent/cover lock drops.

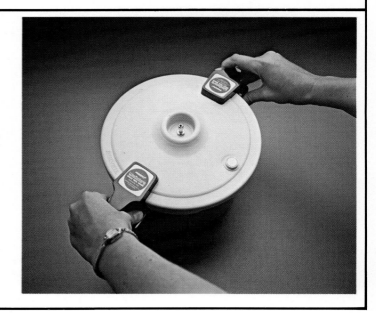

Reducing Pressure

There are three ways to cool the pressure cooker and reduce pressure safely:
1) Cooker can be removed from heat and allowed to cool naturally.
2) Cooker can be removed from heat and held under cold, running water.
3) Cooker can be removed from heat and set in a pan of water.

Sometimes, depending on the recipe, it's best to allow the cooker to cool naturally for a few minutes and then hold it under cold, running water.

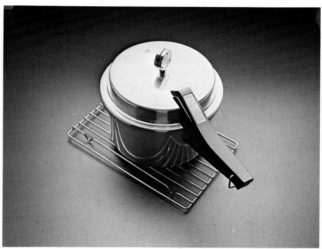

The Vent Tube

It's extremely important that the pressure cooker vent tube not be clogged. You should check it every time you use the cooker by holding the lid up to the light; light should be visible through the tube. If the tube should become clogged, it is easy to clear it by inserting a piece of wire or a pipe cleaner all the way through and pulling it out.

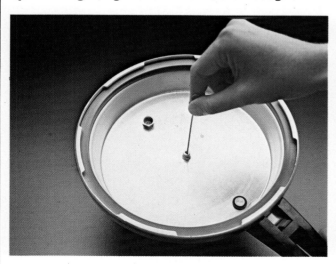

The Gasket

Most pressure cookers have a rubber gasket fitted into a groove in the lid to ensure a tight seal when the cooker is in use. The gasket should be removed, washed and dried, and replaced in the groove after cooking. If the gasket stretches or shrinks, it should be replaced, because the seal the gasket provides is necessary to create pressure in the cooker.

Placing Food In The Cooker

Vegetables and other foods may be cooked by placing them directly in the cooker, with or without the rack, and adding water or other liquid. Meats and poultry will look and taste better, however, if they are browned in butter or vegetable oil in the cooker before the cooking liquid is added. Rinsing the cooker after browning meat is usually unnecessary. But you may want to remove the meat and replace it on the rack.

Cooking Containers

Casseroles, custards, puddings and breads can all be steamed to perfection in the pressure cooker in various kinds of oven-proof containers. It is very important that there be a space of at least ¾ inch between the container and the sides of the cooker to allow steam to circulate. The size and shape of the container, as well as whether it is glass, ceramic or metal, will affect cooking time—ceramic being the slowest heat conductor, metal the fastest. You can use any oven-proof container that fits properly in your pressure cooker but you may have to adjust the timing of a recipe accordingly. Cover containers with foil and either pinch edges to seal or tie with string, as directed in recipe, to secure. Steamed foods are always cooked on the rack. Whether you add water before or after placing containers on the rack is simply a matter of convenience—if the container is large, it's easier to add water first. Tin cans are especially good for steaming cylindrical loaves of bread—always add amount of water specified to maintain sufficient steam.

Pressure Frying

Low-pressure deep frying should never be attempted in a regular pressure cooker. Low-pressure fryers are specially designed for deep-fat frying and they require techniques different from regular cookers. Pour vegetable oil into the low-pressure fryer up to the oil level line marked in

your cooker and heat the oil over high heat to the temperature indicated in the recipe (usually 350°F). Use a deep fat thermometer to check the temperature of the oil. Place prepared food gently in the oil, using tongs or a slotted spoon. If a recipe recommends that you brown the food first, leave the food in the hot oil, uncovered, for the amount of time specified. Then reduce heat and cover the cooker. Start counting pressure-frying minutes from the time cooker is covered; do not wait for pressure to be reached. When cooking has been completed, turn off heat and remove stove-top models from burner. Using a long-tined fork, lift the pressure regulator slightly, without removing it, until pressure has been completely reduced. Then open cooker and remove food with tongs or a slotted spoon.

Stocks and Soups

THERE IS NO more appropriate way to begin using your pressure cooker than with recipes for "homemade" stocks and soups. You may never open a can again! For the pressure cooker creates the best "made-from scratch" soups we've ever tasted — and in not much more time than it takes to heat prepared products.

You'll be especially impressed by the stocks and soups made with beef, chicken or fish bones. There's something almost magical about the capacity of superheated steam to extract maximum flavor by dissolving the rich proteins and other nutrients found in bones. Pressure-cooked stocks compare favorably to those simmered conventionally for hours.

The pressure cooker also displays two other talents specifically useful in soup preparation. The first of these involve vegetables: When you want the flavors of several vegetables to dissolve in a liquid or when you want to achieve a silky-smooth purée, the superheated steam does a splendid job of breaking down the vegetable fibers quickly and uniformly. The second talent significantly reduces the time required to make bean and lentil soups: With the pressure cooker, you don't have to presoak dried beans.

Basic Stocks

We begin this chapter with recipes for three basic stocks — beef, fish, and chicken — because they have so many uses in other recipes. They serve as the base for many other soups; they will enhance meat, chicken and fish entrées when substituted for water as the cooking liquid; and you can make vegetables and rice sparkle simply by steaming these in stock rather than water. Moreover, you can put together a very fast hot lunch or dinner first course by heating stock with noodles and leftover meats and vegetables. Stocks will keep refrigerated in covered jars for two weeks or frozen in covered jars or freezer containers for up to four months. If you freeze stock in ice cube trays, you'll have "instant" stock cubes on hand for up to two months; you can always dissolve these in the water or wine called for in a pressure cooking recipe to add a fillip of flavor.

Vegetable Soups

We use two techniques to bring out the pressure cooker's prowess with vegetable soups.

In recipes for Broccoli Soup, Carrot Potage, Cold Cauliflower Soup and others, we use the pressure cooker in combination with a food processor or blender to create velvety cream soups. The vegetables are puréed either before or after pressure cooking depending on their natural texture and the desired consistency.

In stew-like types of soups, such as Portuguese Soup, it's the varied textures of many ingredients, rather than smooth consistency, that makes the steaming bowlfuls so appealing. We pressure cook these in two or more steps, so that some of the ingredients blend into the thick liquid base, while others cook a shorter amount of time to retain succulence.

Bean And Lentil Soups

The Minestrone and Lentil Soups in this chapter follow other soup techniques except for one difference. For these, we parcook the dried legumes by combining them with water, salt and vegetable oil, cooking them until pressure is reached and then reducing pressure naturally by removing the cooker from the heat and letting it stand. For the Minestrone Soup, you have to cook the dried navy beans again, after they've been parcooked, before adding the other ingredients; with lentils, this step is not necessary. Because all dried legumes tend to produce foam that might clog the vent tube, you should always take these precautions when cooking them: Add one tablespoon of vegetable oil to the water for each cup of beans and lentils both when parcooking them and again when using them in the recipe. And always rinse out the cooker, dry it and check the vent tube after the parcooking step.

Basic Beef Stock

Cook under pressure at 15 lbs. for 40 minutes.

You can make a rich stock in a matter of minutes in the pressure cooker. Keep it frozen in small containers until you're ready to use it in soups or sauces.

1 tablespoon vegetable oil
2½ to 3 pounds meaty soup bones
2 large carrots, cut into 1-inch pieces
2 stalks celery, cut into 2-inch pieces
1 small onion, peeled and cut into small cubes
1 turnip or rutabaga, peeled and cubed
1 quart water
½ cup chopped parsley
½ teaspoon dried oregano leaves
⅛ teaspoon curry, if desired
1 teaspoon salt
4 peppercorns
½ teaspoon sugar

1. Heat oil in cooker. Place washed soup bones, carrots, celery, onion and turnip in cooker, sauté until brown. Add remaining ingredients.

2. Cover and set control at 15. Cook over high heat until pressure is reached. Reduce heat; cook 40 minutes.

3. Cool cooker naturally 5 minutes; complete pressure reduction by placing cooker under cold, running water.

4. Strain stock through a fine sieve or double thickness cheesecloth.

5. Refrigerate stock until fat solidifies on top; skim off fat.

Makes about 1 quart

Tip:

For delicate color and flavor, place meat bones for stock in pressure cooker, cover with water and bring to a boil; then drain bones, rinse under cold water and proceed with recipe. For deep, rich color, brown meat bones in pressure cooker before adding other ingredients.

Basic Fish Stock

Cook under pressure at 15 lbs. for 15 minutes.

With fish stock on hand, you are always ready to create both delicate sauces and aspics and hearty chowders.

3 tablespoons butter or margarine
⅓ cup onions, peeled and chopped
⅓ cup carrots, diced
⅓ cup celery, chopped
1 pound washed fish bones, heads, tails, including skin
1 teaspoon salt
¼ teaspoon white pepper
1 sprig parsley
½ bay leaf
1 teaspoon dried thyme leaves
2 cloves
⅓ cup dry white wine
2 cups cold water

1. Heat butter in cooker; add onions, carrots, and celery and cook over low heat until just tender. Add remaining ingredients.

2. Cover and set control at 15. Cook over high heat until pressure is reached. Reduce heat; cook 15 minutes.

3. Cool cooker naturally 5 minutes; place cooker under cold, running water to complete pressure reduction.

4. Strain stock through fine sieve or double thickness cheesecloth.

Makes about 2 cups

Basic Chicken Stock

Cook under pressure at 15 lbs. for 15 minutes.

Golden, flavorful chicken stock may be served plain as a broth, used in sauces or casseroles, or combined with vegetables, noodles or rice for a hearty soup.

1½ pounds chicken pieces (wings, neck, back, gizzard, heart, scraps)
1 quart water
1 teaspoon salt
1 onion, peeled and sliced
1 carrot, sliced
1 stalk celery, cut in thirds
2 tablespoons sherry
1½ tablespoons vegetable oil

1. Wipe chicken pieces with damp cloth and dry; place in cooker and add water.

2. Add salt, onion and carrot.

3. Wash celery and add to mixture.

4. Bring to a boil uncovered. Skim foam off top. Add sherry and oil.

5. Cover and set control at 15. Cook over high heat until pressure is reached. Reduce heat; cook 15 minutes.

6. Cool cooker naturally 5 minutes; place cooker under cold, running water to complete pressure reduction.

7. Strain stock through fine sieve or double thickness cheesecloth.

Makes about 1 quart

Variations: Serve as a cold jellied broth. Or add 2 cups diced vegetables of choice. For Chicken Noodle Soup, add ²/₃ cup noodles and boil, uncovered, for 12 to 15 minutes.

Tip:
Stocks will keep refrigerated in covered jars for two weeks; they will keep frozen in covered jars or freezer containers for four months. You can also freeze stock in ice cube trays for up to two months for convenient use of small amounts.

Fast and Easy Zucchini Soup

Cook under pressure at 15 lbs. for 2 minutes.

This popular summer soup takes only about 5 minutes to prepare and may be served either hot or cold.

1 medium zucchini, sliced
1 cup beef stock (or 1 can 10½ ounces beef broth)
⅓ cup milk or half and half
½ teaspoon dried tarragon leaves
½ teaspoon salt
⅛ teaspoon white pepper

1. Place half of the zucchini slices, the stock and milk in blender or food processor; process until zucchini is finely chopped. Repeat procedure with remaining zucchini, stock and milk. Pour zucchini mixture, tarragon, salt and pepper into cooker.

2. Cover and set control at 15. Cook over high heat until pressure is reached. Reduce heat; cook 2 minutes.

3. Cool cooker naturally 5 minutes; place cooker under cold, running water to reduce pressure completely.

4. Serve soup hot or cold.

Makes 2 servings

Garden Vegetable Soup

Cook under pressure at 15 lbs. for 6 minutes.

This soup is great for days when you want to serve a hot lunch in a hurry. You'll find it a filling one-pot meal.

2 tablespoons vegetable oil
½ pound lean beef chuck, cut into ½-inch cubes
1 potato, pared, cut into ¼-inch cubes
½ onion, coarsely chopped
2 medium carrots, cut into ½-inch cubes
2 large stalks celery, cut into 2-inch slices
1 cup fresh or canned tomatoes, coarsely chopped
1 cup fresh or frozen green beans, cut into 1-inch pieces
½ cup dry red wine
3½ cups beef stock
1 teaspoon dried oregano leaves
1 teaspoon dried thyme leaves
1 clove garlic, minced
½ teaspoon curry powder
2 teaspoons salt
1 teaspoon pepper

1. Heat oil in cooker; brown meat cubes on all sides. Add remaining ingredients.

2. Cover and set control at 15. Cook over high heat until pressure is reached. Reduce heat; cook 6 minutes.

3. Cool cooker naturally 5 minutes; complete pressure reduction by placing cooker under cold, running water.

Makes 4 to 6 servings

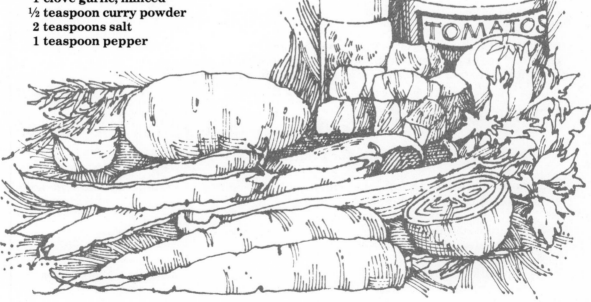

Tips:
You can prepare any of your own favorite recipes for stocks and soups in the pressure cooker; they will require about one-third of the normal cooking time.

Always check the vent tube by holding the cover up to the light before using pressure cooker; light should be visible through the tube.

Broccoli Soup

Cook under pressure at 15 lbs. for 2 minutes.

Filled with eye-appeal and fresh flavor, Broccoli Soup may be served hot or cold.

½ **pound fresh broccoli,**
    trimmed of outer leaves
    and tough stems
1 **cup water**
½ **teaspoon salt**
2 **to 3 cups chicken stock**
⅛ **teaspoon ground nutmeg**
¼ **cup whipping cream or milk**
¼ **cup whipping cream,**
    whipped
    Paprika

1. Wash and place prepared broccoli in cooker. Add water and salt.

2. Cover and set control at 15. Cook over high heat until pressure is reached. Reduce heat; cook 2 minutes.

3. Reduce pressure at once by placing cooker under cold, running water.

4. Purée half the broccoli and cooking liquid in food processor or blender. Repeat with remaining broccoli and liquid. Place broccoli in cooker; stir in chicken stock to consistency desired; stir in nutmeg.

5. Heat broccoli mixture, uncovered, over medium heat to simmering. Reduce heat to low. Pour in cream or milk. Cook, stirring occasionally, for about 3 minutes.

6. Pour soup into bowls or tureen. Garnish with dollops of whipped cream, and sprinkle with paprika.

Makes 4 to 6 servings

Bonga Bonga Soup

Cook under pressure at 15 lbs. for 0 minutes.

This quick home version of Trader Vic's restaurant specialty is bound to please with its creamy blend of flavors.

1 **pound fresh spinach or 1**
    package (10 ounces) frozen
    chopped spinach
¾ **cup water**
1 **can (10½ ounces) oyster stew**
1 **tablespoon dry white wine, if**
    desired
1 **teaspoon instant onion**
½ **teaspoon salt**
¼ **teaspoon white pepper**
¼ **cup cream, lightly whipped**
    Paprika

1. Wash spinach thoroughly under running water and cut off stems. Place spinach and water in cooker.

2. Cover and set control at 15. Cook over high heat until pressure is reached. Cook 0 minutes. Remove cooker from heat.

3. Reduce pressure at once by placing cooker under cold, running water.

4. Measure spinach and liquid to make 2 cups. Purée in food processor or blender.

5. Add remaining ingredients except whipped cream and paprika; purée. (If mixture is thicker than you desire, add milk.)

6. Heat mixture over medium-low heat, until hot; do not boil.

7. Pour soup into a tureen or individual soup bowls, spoon whipped cream over top and sprinkle with paprika.

Makes 4 servings

Manhattan Clam Chowder

Cook under pressure at 15 lbs. for 6 minutes.

Manhattan Clam Chowder is an East Coast cousin of the creamy New England Chowder, but tomatoes and herbs give it a quite different flavor.

3 tablespoons butter or
    margarine
3 slices bacon, cut into 1-inch
    pieces
½ cup thinly-sliced red onion
1 cup pared, diced potato
1 green pepper, finely chopped
2 stalks celery, washed and cut
    into ¼-inch slices
1 clove garlic, minced
1 teaspoon salt
⅛ teaspoon white pepper
1½ cups clam juice or fish stock
½ cup dry white wine
2 cups canned, whole tomatoes,
    seeded, chopped
½ teaspoon dried oregano
    leaves
½ teaspoon dried thyme leaves
2 cups minced clams
    Grated Parmesan cheese, if
    desired

1. Melt butter in cooker. Add bacon, onion, potato, green pepper, celery, garlic, salt and pepper and cook until onion is tender.

2. Add clam juice, wine, tomatoes, oregano and thyme.

3. Cover and set control at 15. Cook over high heat until pressure is reached. Reduce heat; cook 6 minutes.

4. Cool cooker naturally 5 minutes; place cooker under cold, running water to complete pressure reduction.

5. Add clams; heat to boiling. Reduce heat; simmer 2 minutes. Pour into soup bowls or tureen. Serve with Parmesan cheese, if desired.

Makes 4 servings

Leek Soup

Cook under pressure at 15 lbs. for 0 minutes.

Leeks are the national emblem of Wales and a favorite of soup lovers everywhere.

6 leeks
2 cups water
2 cups chicken stock
1 tablespoon butter or
    margarine
1 cup whipping cream
1 teaspoon salt
⅛ teaspoon white pepper
⅛ teaspoon sugar
    Chopped parsley

1. Trim green tops from leeks and slice thin to make ¼ cup. Reserve for garnish.

2. Remove root tips and cut leeks in half lengthwise. Wash leeks thoroughly under cold, running water. Slice thin to make 4 cups.

3. Place 4 cups leeks, the water, chicken stock and butter in cooker.

4. Cover and set control at 15. Cook over high heat until pressure is reached. Cook 0 minutes. Remove cooker from heat.

5. Reduce pressure at once by placing cooker under cold, running water.

6. Stir in cream, salt, pepper and sugar. Serve hot or cold; garnish with leek tops and parsley.

Makes 6 servings

New England Clam Chowder

Simmer clams until shells open, about 10 minutes.

Cook under pressure at 15 lbs. for 4 minutes.

This chowder has a proud history, as clams were used by New England's early settlers. Because milk tends to scorch easily when pressure cooked, we add it at the end and simmer the soup briefly in an uncovered cooker on top of the range.

18 large fresh clams (or 2 cups canned, minced)
Water (enough to cover)
¼ pound salt pork, cut into ½-inch cubes
1 onion, sliced thin
2 potatoes, pared and diced
Boiling water
1 teaspoon paprika
⅛ teaspoon white pepper
¼ teaspoon dried dillweed
2 tablespoons shredded Swiss cheese
2 cups milk
4 round water crackers, split in half

1. (If using canned clams, omit steps 1 and 2.) Place fresh, unshelled clams in cooker; cover with water. Heat to boiling; simmer until clams open, about 10 minutes. Drain; cool.

2. Remove clams from shells; chop clams, reserve liquid.

3. Brown salt pork in cooker. Add onion and potatoes; cook 5 minutes, stirring occasionally.

4. Add enough boiling water to clam liquid to make 2 cups. Add to cooker with paprika, pepper, dillweed and cheese. Cover and set control at 15. Cook over high heat until pressure is reached. Reduce heat; cook 4 minutes.

5. Reduce pressure at once by placing cooker under cold, running water.

6. Stir in remaining ingredients; simmer uncovered until mixture begins to thicken, about 5 minutes.
Makes 4 to 6 servings

Cold Cauliflower Soup

Cook under pressure at 15 lbs. for 3 minutes.

Delicate and light in color, this cold cauliflower soup provides a welcome summer first course.

1 large cauliflower
½ cup water
½ teaspoon salt
¼ teaspoon white pepper
1 tablespoon instant onion
2 cups milk
¼ cup dry white wine, if desired
1 teaspoon prepared horseradish
½ cup whipping cream, whipped
Paprika

1. Trim cauliflower of outer leaves; wash and break into flowerets.

2. Place cauliflower, water and salt in cooker.

3. Cover and set control at 15. Cook over high heat until pressure is reached. Reduce heat; cook 3 minutes.

4. Reduce pressure instantly by placing cooker under cold, running water.

5. Purée cauliflower with cooking liquid in blender or food processor. Refrigerate until chilled.

6. Stir in pepper, onion, milk, wine and horseradish; refrigerate ½ hour.

7. Serve in bowls; garnish with dollops of whipped cream; sprinkle with paprika.
Makes 4 to 6 servings

Portuguese Soup

Cook under pressure at 15 lbs. for 25 minutes, and then 1½ minutes more. (See recipe how-to on pages 66-67.)

Coriander gives this hearty beef soup an unusual flavor. Use fresh coriander if you can; it's sometimes called Chinese parsley in the market.

1½ pounds beef brisket, cubed
1 onion, chopped
1 clove garlic, minced
1 quart water
2 cans (8 ounces each) tomato sauce with tomato bits
1 can (8 ounces) golden corn
2 tablespoons chopped parsley
1 teaspoon salt
2 teaspoons crushed fresh coriander or 1 teaspoon dried coriander leaves
⅛ teaspoon pepper
1 small bay leaf
1 large potato, pared, cut into cubes
1 small bunch chard, collards or spinach, torn into small pieces
½ cup dry red wine
4 to 6 slices toasted, buttered French bread

1. In cooker, place beef, onion, garlic, water, tomato sauce, corn, parsley, salt, coriander, pepper and bay leaf.

2. Cover and set control at 15. Cook over high heat until pressure is reached. Reduce heat; cook 25 minutes.

3. Cool cooker naturally 5 minutes; place cooker under cold, running water to complete pressure reduction.

4. Add potato and chard. Cover and set control at 15. Cook over high heat until pressure is reached. Reduce heat; cook 1½ minutes.

5. Cool cooker naturally 5 minutes; place cooker under cold, running water to complete pressure reduction.

6. Stir in wine; heat, uncovered, to simmering. Serve in bowls; place bread slice in each.

Makes 4 to 6 servings

Tip:

Always check the vent tube by holding the cover up to the light before using pressure cooker; light should be visible through the tube.

Carrot Potage

Cook under pressure at 15 lbs. for 1½ minutes. Include an extra 20 minutes to simmer puréed ingredients. (See recipe how-to on pages 65-66.)

This thick carrot soup makes an elegant first course or light luncheon main dish.

6 medium carrots, washed, scraped and sliced
½ teaspoon salt
½ cup water
2 tablespoons butter or margarine
2 tablespoons all-purpose flour
⅛ teaspoon cayenne pepper
2¾ cups warm milk
Minced parsley

1. Place prepared carrots, salt and water in cooker.

2. Cover and set control at 15. Cook over high heat until pressure is reached. Reduce heat; cook 1½ minutes.

3. Reduce pressure at once by placing cooker under cold, running water. Reserve 6 carrot slices for garnish.

4. Purée remaining carrots and liquid in food processor or blender.

5. Heat butter in cooker; stir in flour and cayenne to make a smooth paste. Stir in milk gradually. Cook, stirring constantly, until mixture thickens.

Carrot Potage (Continued)

6. Stir in carrot purée and simmer gently for 20 minutes, stirring occasionally.

7. Pour soup into bowls or tureen; garnish with carrot slices and parsley. Soup may be chilled and served cold.

Makes 4 to 6 servings

Favorite Minestrone

Cook under pressure at 15 lbs. for 0 minutes, and then 25 minutes more plus an extra 4 minutes when all ingredients (except cheese) have been added.

This fragrant minestrone has a lovely consistency — neither too thick or too thin. We parcook the dried beans instead of soaking them overnight to save time.

2 cups dried navy beans
4 cups water
2 tablespoons vegetable oil
6 cups water
2 teaspoons salt
1 tablespoon vegetable oil
2 ounces salt pork, cut into ¼ inch cubes
2 cloves garlic, minced
1 small onion, coarsely chopped
2 tablespoons minced parsley
2 teaspoons chopped fresh basil or 1 teaspoon dried basil leaves
1 teaspoon dried oregano leaves
1 bay leaf
2 cups chopped tomatoes
1 cup finely-chopped zucchini
1 cup peeled, cubed potatoes
½ cup finely-shredded cabbage
1 teaspoon salt
4 to 6 whole cloves
1 cup uncooked elbow macaroni
½ cup grated Parmesan cheese

1. Place beans, 4 cups water and 2 tablespoons oil in cooker. Cover and set control at 15. Cook over high heat until pressure is reached. Remove cooker from heat. Cool cooker naturally. Drain beans. Rinse out cooker and dry.

2. Place drained, par-cooked beans in cooker; add 6 cups water, 2 teaspoons salt and 1 tablespoon oil.

3. Cover and set control at 15. Cook over high heat until pressure is reached. Reduce heat; cook 25 minutes.

4. Cool cooker naturally 5 minutes; place cooker under cold, running water to complete pressure reduction. Drain beans; reserve liquid.

5. Place salt pork, garlic, onion, parsley and basil in cooker; cook stirring occasionally, until salt pork is brown.

6. Add beans, broth and remaining ingredients, except cheese.

7. Cover and set control at 15. Cook over high heat until pressure is reached. Reduce heat; cook 4 minutes.

8. Cool cooker naturally 5 minutes; place cooker under cold running water to complete pressure reduction.

9. Pour soup into tureen or soup bowls; sprinkle with cheese.

Makes 6 to 8 servings

Tips:

If you have a 6-quart or larger pressure cooker, you can double the amounts specified in stock and soup recipes. Never fill cooker more than two-thirds or three-fourths full, according to manufacturer's recommendation.

When cooking beans or lentils, be sure to add one tablespoon of vegetable oil for each cup of beans to prevent frothing.

Waterfront Cioppino

Cook under pressure at 15 lbs. for 10 minutes.

San Francisco's Italian community is renowned for their classic and succulent Cioppino. This version is easier to shop for, less expensive and more quickly prepared, but it is every bit as delicious. Serve it with thick slices of Italian bread.

1 tablespoon olive or vegetable oil
1 cup chopped green pepper
1½ cups chopped onion
1½ cups chopped celery
2 cloves garlic, minced
1 large carrot, diagonally sliced
1 can (16 ounces) whole tomatoes, undrained
2 cans (6 ounces each) tomato paste
1 bay leaf
¾ teaspoon dried basil leaves
1 teaspoon salt
¼ teaspoon pepper
1 pound frozen perch or seabass fillets, slightly thawed
1 pint fish stock
6 ounces canned clams
½ pound raw shrimps or prawns, shelled and deveined
¼ cup dry sherry

1. Heat oil in cooker. Sauté green pepper, onion, celery and garlic until onion is tender. Add carrot, tomatoes and liquid and tomato paste, seasonings, perch and fish stock. Add water if a thinner mixture is desired.

2. Cover and set control at 15. Cook over high heat until pressure is reached. Reduce heat, cook 10 minutes.

3. Cool cooker naturally 5 minutes; place cooker under cold, running water to complete pressure reduction.

4. Add clams, shrimp and sherry. Simmer uncovered, 5 minutes.

Makes 4 servings

Russian Borscht

Cook under pressure at 15 lbs. for 30 minutes, and then 3 ½ minutes more.

The chef in a small, excellent restaurant near the Kiov Theatre in Leningrad refused to share his recipe with us, but we vowed we'd try to reproduce it. So here it is!

1 pound boneless chuck, fat trimmed, cut into small cubes
1½ quarts water
1½ teaspoons salt
1 can (16 ounces) beets, undrained
2 tablespoons tomato paste
¾ cup shredded carrots
¾ cup shredded rutabagas
1 cup shredded cabbage
2 tablespoons vinegar

1. Place meat, water, salt in cooker. Cover and set control at 15. Cook over high heat until pressure is reached. Reduce heat. Cook 30 minutes.

2. Cool cooker naturally 5 minutes; complete pressure reduction by placing cooker under cold, running water.

3. Skim fat from surface of broth.

4. Puree beets and liquid and tomato paste in food processor or blender; add to soup.

5. Stir in remaining ingredients except sour cream.

Russian Borscht (Continued)

1 tablespoon butter or
   margarine
1 bay leaf
   Sour cream, if desired

6. Cover and set control at 15. Cook over high heat until pressure is reached. Reduce heat; cook 3½ minutes.

7. Cool cooker naturally 5 minutes; place cooker under cold, running water to complete pressure reduction.

8. Pour soup into bowls; garnish with dollops of sour cream.

Makes 6 to 8 servings

Variation: Add 1 can beer after cooking, reheat in uncovered cooker.

Ruby Red Soup

Cook under pressure at 15 lbs. for 40 minutes, and then 3 minutes more.

Beef provides this tomato soup with a wonderful richness and cumin adds unique piquancy. Serve it steaming with hunks of crusty French bread.

2 pounds beef knuckle, cracked
1 pound beef chuck or brisket,
   cut into small cubes
2 quarts water
2 teaspoons salt
2 tablespoons instant onion
½ cup chopped parsley
2 stalks celery, cut in 2-inch
   slices
1 carrot, scraped and sliced
   into ¼-inch slices
4 whole peppercorns
6 cups fresh or canned ripe
   tomatoes, peeled and
   chopped
1 teaspoon ground cumin or 1½
   teaspoons dried basil
   leaves
¼ cup wine vinegar

1. Place all ingredients except tomatoes, cumin and vinegar in cooker.

2. Cover and set control at 15. Cook over high heat until pressure is reached. Reduce heat; cook 40 minutes.

3. Cool cooker naturally 5 minutes; place cooker under cold, running water to complete pressure reduction. Remove bone and skim fat from broth.

4. Add remaining ingredients to cooker.

5. Cover and set control at 15. Cook over high heat until pressure is reached. Reduce heat; cook 3 minutes.

6. Reduce pressure at once by placing cooker under cold, running water.

7. Strain soup through coarse sieve or double layer cheesecloth. Return soup to cooker; heat over medium heat, stirring occasionally, until hot.

Makes 8 servings

Tips:

Always check the vent tube by holding the cover up to the light before using pressure cooker; light should be visible through the tube.

If you have a 6-quart or larger pressure cooker, you can double the amounts specified in stock and soup recipes. Never fill cooker more than two-thirds or three-fourths full, according to manufacturer's recommendation.

Lentil Soup

Cook under pressure at 15 lbs. for 0 minutes, and then 14 minutes more.

Ham gives this hearty, robust lentil soup a mild, smokey flavor. Add oil to lentils to reduce frothing and wash and check the vent pipe after cooking.

1 cup dried lentils
2 cups water
1 teaspoon salt
1 tablespoon vegetable oil
2 tablespoons butter or margarine
¼ pound ham, cut into small cubes, or 1 ham bone
½ cup minced onion
2 tablespoons vegetable oil
½ cup chopped celery
½ cup finely-chopped carrots
1 clove garlic, minced
1 bay leaf, crumbled
2 cups water
Seasoned Croutons (recipe follows)

1. Place lentils, 2 cups water, salt and 1 tablespoon oil in cooker.
2. Cover and set control at 15. Cook over high heat until pressure is reached. Remove cooker from heat. Reduce pressure naturally. Drain lentils. Rinse cooker and wipe dry.
3. Heat butter in cooker; cook ham until light brown. Remove ham. Add onion; sauté in 2 tablespoons oil until tender. Stir in lentils and remaining ingredients.
4. Cover and set control at 15. Cook over high heat until pressure is reached. Reduce heat; cook 14 minutes.
5. Cool cooker naturally 5 minutes; place cooker under cold, running water to complete pressure reduction.
6. Make Seasoned Croutons (recipe follows).
7. Serve in soup bowls or tureen; sprinkle with croutons.

Makes 4 servings

Variations: Garlic, finely minced, may be increased or omitted as desired. Add finely-ground Parmesan cheese, if you wish. Or sprinkle cheese over soup at the table.

Seasoned Croutons

1½ teaspoons butter or margarine
2 slices white or whole wheat bread, crusts trimmed, cut into cubes
½ teaspoon salt
½ teaspoon paprika
Grated Parmesan cheese or ½ teaspoon toasted sesame seeds

1. Heat butter in cooker or in skillet; add bread cubes.
2. Sauté, stirring constantly, until bread is brown on all sides.
3. Sprinkle remaining ingredients over bread; toss to coat.

Makes 4 servings

Tips:
When cooking beans or lentils, be sure to add one tablespoon of vegetable oil for each cup of beans to prevent frothing.

If you have a 6-quart or larger pressure cooker, you can double the amounts specified in stock and soup recipes. Never fill cooker more than two-thirds or three-fourths full, according to manufacturer's recommendation.

Fruktsoppa
(Old~Fashioned Fruit Soup)

Cook under pressure at 15 lbs. for 6 minutes. Include an extra 10 minutes to simmer fruit.

A cold Scandinavian fruit soup makes a refreshing beginning or ending for a hot-weather meal.

¼ cup dried apricots
¾ cup dried prunes
¼ cup dried peaches, cut in halves
¼ cup dried pears, cut in halves
6 cups cold water
1 cinnamon stick
2 lemon slices, cut thickly
2 tablespoons quick-cooking tapioca
3 tablespoons sugar or honey
2 tablespoons raisins
1 tablespoon dried currants
1 green apple, pared and cut into ½-inch slices

1. Wash and soak apricots, prunes, peaches and pears in water 30 minutes. Pour fruit and water into cooker.

2. Cover and set control at 15. Cook over high heat until pressure is reached. Reduce heat; cook 6 minutes.

3. Cool cooker naturally 5 minutes; complete pressure reduction by placing cooker under cold, running water.

4. Add cinnamon stick, lemon slices and tapioca; heat to boiling, stirring occasionally.

5. Stir in remaining ingredients. Simmer, uncovered, until fruit is tender but not mushy, about 10 minutes. Remove lemon and cinnamon stick. Refrigerate until chilled.

6. Serve the soup in chilled bowls or in compote dishes if used as a dessert.

Makes 4 to 6 servings

Cold Curried Apple Soup

Cook under pressure at 5 lbs. for 2 minutes (or at 15 lbs. for 1 minute).

There's a delightful and refreshing taste of the Far East in this chilled apple-curry blend. Peak its flavor with a sprinkling of cinnamon.

2 tablespoons butter or margarine
1 tablespoon curry powder
¼ cup flour
1 cup chicken stock
1 cup apple juice
1 apple, pared, cored, cubed
1 cup whipping cream
Cinnamon

1. Melt butter in cooker; stir in curry; sauté 1 minute, stirring constantly.

2. Stir in flour to make a smooth paste. Remove from heat; stir in chicken stock gradually. Stir in apple juice and half the apple.

3. Cover and set control at 5. Cook over high heat until pressure is reached. Reduce heat; cook 2 minutes (at 15 pounds pressure, cook 1 minute).

4. Cool cooker naturally 5 minutes; place cooker under cold, running water to reduce pressure completely.

5. Refrigerate soup until chilled. Stir in remaining apples and cream. Sprinkle lightly with cinnamon.

Makes 2 to 4 servings

Meat

WHEN YOU PREPARE meat recipes in the pressure cooker, you'll notice that the aroma of the cooking food is even more intense and more savory than with other methods, and this will prove an accurate clue to the quality of the finished dish. Any meat that can be braised, stewed, steamed or simmered conventionally will cook beautifully in the pressure cooker in a fraction of the usual time.

Shoppers at the meat counter usually have to choose between expensive meats that can be broiled or roasted with minimum of effort and economical cuts that require elaborate and time-consuming preparation. The pressure cooker resolves a good part of this dilemma by making it possible to turn out Beef Stew with Yogurt, for example, in 12 to 15 minutes or Fruited Pot Roast in an hour or less.

The precise cooking time a recipe requires depends on several factors. Although even the same size pieces of beef, lamb, pork and veal would take different amounts of time to cook, the most important distinction in pressure cooking is the thickness of the pieces of meat. So if you're using a cut of meat thinner than specified in a recipe, you should reduce the cooking time. If the cut or the pieces of meat are thicker, increase the cooking time. You can always check the meat for doneness by removing the cooker from the heat, reducing pressure as specified in the recipe, and testing the meat for tenderness with a fork. If the meat isn't quite done, make sure there is sufficient liquid in the pot to continue pressure cooking; then close the cooker, bring it back up to pressure and cook longer.

As with any other kind of meat cookery, there are diverse opinions on the proper temperature to use when pressure cooking meats. Many cooks prefer lower temperatures — the theory being that less moisture will be lost. In pressure cooking, this means regulating the pressure at 10 pounds or 238°F (114°C) instead of 15 pounds or 250°F (121°C). Because pressure-cooked meats retain natural juices either way, and because cooking times are never very long, we don't feel that the difference in pressure level is significant. If you pre-fer to cook at 10 pounds pressure, the recipes will take a few minutes longer.

Browning Meat

It's almost always preferable to brown beef, lamb, veal or pork before pressure cooking it for best flavor and appearance. You can accomplish this step in the open cooker lightly greased with butter or vegetable oil. Often the meat is lightly coated with flour before browning for enhanced flavor and appearance but you can dispense with this step if you're counting calories. You needn't rinse out the cooker after browning the meat; sometimes you do have to lift out the meat to place the rack in the cooker before proceeding with the recipe.

Marinades And Cooking Liquids

Zesty marinades improve the flavor of such entrées as Sauerbraten, Barbecued Short Ribs and Polynesian Pork. These meats should be allowed to marinate, refrigerated, at least as long as the recipe specifies. Even if the time specified is only a few hours, you may find it convenient to mix the marinade a day ahead of time and allow the meat to absorb extra flavor overnight. When meats have been marinated, we use the marinade as the cooking liquid needed for pressure cooking.

Sometimes the flavor of the cooking liquid doesn't affect the finished dish, and in these recipes water is the only liquid you need. More often than not, however, stock, wine, beer, vegetable and fruit juices, or bouillon yield better results. You can substitute one liquid for another, but always use the full volume specified. The cooking liquid left in the cooker after the meat has cooked can form the base for a variety of savory sauces. Often all it takes to make a delicious sauce from the seasoned wine, stock or juice is flour, cornstarch, or arrowroot for thickening. You can mix and simmer the sauce right in the cooker. Sometimes the cooking liquid itself, perhaps enriched with a little butter or simply reduced by rapid boiling, is sufficiently well-seasoned to serve as a gravy.

Savory Round Steak

Cook under pressure at 15 lbs. for 13 minutes.

Herbs, wine, vegetables and quick pressure cooking turn economical round steak into a tender, savory entrée.

1½ pounds round steak, 1-inch thick, cut into 4 pieces
3 tablespoons all-purpose flour
2 tablespoons vegetable oil
1 medium onion, chopped
4 ounces sliced mushrooms
4 carrots, cut in 1-inch pieces
½ cup tomato juice
¼ cup dry red wine
1 tablespoon dehydrated parsley flakes
1 teaspoon salt
2 teaspoons Worcestershire sauce
½ teaspoon oregano
¼ teaspoon pepper
1 bay leaf
¼ cup cold water
2 tablespoons all-purpose flour

1. Coat steak with 3 tablespoons flour and cook on both sides in oil until browned. Remove from cooker.

2. Cook onion and mushrooms in drippings until lightly browned, 2 to 3 minutes.

3. Return steak to cooker. Add all remaining ingredients except cold water and 2 tablespoons flour.

4. Cover and set control at 15. Cook over high heat until pressure is reached. Reduce heat; cook 13 minutes.

5. Cool cooker naturally 5 minutes; place cooker under cold, running water to complete pressure reduction.

6. Remove steak and vegetables to serving platter; keep warm. Discard bay leaf.

7. Mix cold water and 2 tablespoons flour. Stir into liquid in cooker. Bring to boil. Cook, stirring constantly, until thickened, 1 to 2 minutes.

Makes 4 servings

Beef Stew with Yogurt

Cook under pressure at 10 lbs. for 10 minutes (or at 15 lbs. for 8 minutes).

This hearty dish probably originated in Scandinavia. It has become standard fare in many American homes for good reason — the allspice and yogurt give the stew a special zest.

2 pounds boneless beef chuck, cut into 1½-inch cubes
1 tablespoon all-purpose flour
½ teaspoon salt
1½ tablespoons butter or margarine
1 large onion, sliced paper thin
½ teaspoon ground allspice
1 bay leaf, crumbled
1¼ cups beef stock
¼ cup yogurt or sour cream

1. Coat meat with flour; sprinkle with salt. Heat butter in cooker; cook meat until brown on all sides. Add onion, allspice, bay leaf, and stock.

2. Cover and set control at 10. Cook over high heat until pressure is reached. Reduce heat; cook 10 minutes (at 15 pounds pressure, cook 8 minutes).

3. Cool cooker naturally 5 minutes; place cooker under cold, running water to complete pressure reduction.

4. Spoon meat onto serving platter. Stir yogurt into liquid in cooker; heat over low heat 2 to 3 minutes. Serve over meat.

Makes 4 servings

Sauerbraten with Potato Dumplings

Marinate meat for 24 to 48 hours before cooking.

Cook under pressure at 10 lbs. for 45 minutes (or at 15 lbs. for 35 minutes). Include an extra 10 minutes to simmer dumplings.

The longer you marinate the meat, the tangier this German specialty will be. Simmer Potato Dumplings in the cooking liquid before you make the gravy.

3 pounds beef rump roast
1 cup cider vinegar
⅔ cup sliced onion
1 cup water
1 clove garlic, minced
1 bay leaf, crumbled
4 whole cloves
½ teaspoon ground allspice
1 teaspoon salt
⅛ teaspoon pepper
1 tablespoon sugar
½ teaspoon mustard seeds
2 tablespoons all-purpose flour
¼ teaspoon salt
⅛ teaspoon pepper
2 tablespoons vegetable oil
   Water (see Preparation)
6 gingersnaps, crumbled
1 cup yogurt or sour cream
   Potato Dumplings (recipe
   follows)

1. Wipe pot roast with damp cloth; pat dry with paper towel. Place meat in a large bowl.

2. Heat vinegar, onion, water, garlic, bay leaf, cloves, allspice, 1 teaspoon salt, ⅛ teaspoon pepper, the sugar and mustard seeds to boiling. Pour hot mixture over meat; refrigerate 1 to 2 days, turning meat two or three times.

3. Drain; reserve liquid. Dry meat on paper towel.

4. Combine flour, ¼ teaspoon salt and ⅛ teaspoon pepper; coat meat on all sides. Heat 2 tablespoons oil in cooker; cook meat until brown on all surfaces.

5. Place meat on rack in cooker. Measure reserved marinade; add water to make 2 cups; add to cooker.

6. Cover and set control at 10. Cook over high heat until pressure is reached. Reduce heat; cook 45 minutes (at 15 pounds pressure; cook 35 minutes).

7. Cool cooker naturally 5 minutes; place cooker under cold, running water to complete pressure reduction.

8. Place meat on serving platter; keep warm. Remove rack from cooker.

9. Make Potato Dumplings (recipe follows).

10. Stir gingersnaps and yogurt into cooking liquid; cook 2 to 3 minutes. Serve sauce over meat.

Makes 6 servings

Potato Dumplings

1 pound medium potatoes,
   boiled and peeled
3 eggs
1 cup all-purpose flour
1 teaspoon salt
   Dash white pepper
   Dash nutmeg

1. Mash potatoes; blend in eggs, flour, salt, pepper and nutmeg.

2. Pinch off pieces of potato mixture and roll into 1-inch balls.

3. Bring liquid in cooker to boil. Drop potato balls into boiling water. Cook until they float to surface; then reduce heat and simmer 5 minutes. Remove dumplings to serving platter with meat. Make sauce as directed above.

Tongue with Madeira Sauce

Cook under pressure at 10 lbs. for 60 minutes (or at 15 lbs. for 45 to 50 minutes). Include an extra 20 minutes to simmer Madeira Sauce.

Cured tongue is particularly tasty when prepared in a pressure cooker. Serve hot with Madeira Sauce and buttered noodles, or cold with a sweet-sour Mustard Sauce and potato salad.

1 cured tongue, about 3 pounds
1 bay leaf, crumbled
¼ teaspoon fines herbes
1 tablespoon instant minced onion
1 stalk celery
3 peppercorns
4 cloves
2 cups water
1 cup Madeira Sauce (recipe follows) or Mustard Sauce (recipe follows)

1. Wipe tongue with damp cloth; pat dry with paper towel. Trim thick or loose pieces from tongue; place tongue in cooker. Add remaining ingredients except sauces.

2. Cover cooker; set control at 10. Cook over high heat until pressure is reached. Reduce heat; cook 1 hour (at 15 pounds pressure, cook 45 to 50 minutes).

3. Cool cooker naturally 5 minutes; place cooker under cold, running water to complete pressure reduction.

4. Reserve 1 cup cooking liquid for Madeira Sauce.

5. Peel skin from tongue; keep tongue warm.

6. Make Madeira Sauce or Mustard Sauce (recipes follow).

7. Slice tongue and arrange on serving platter. Serve with choice of sauce.

Makes 6 to 8 servings

Madeira Sauce

3 tablespoons butter or margarine, melted
1 tablespoon all-purpose flour
1 cup reserved liquid from cooker
2 tablespoons Madeira wine
¼ teaspoon wine vinegar
⅛ teaspoon fines herbes

1. Melt 3 tablespoons butter in cooker. Stir in flour; cook until golden.

2. Stir in reserved cooking liquid; cook, stirring constantly, until sauce thickens. Simmer 20 minutes.

3. Remove cooker from heat; stir in wine, vinegar and fines herbes.

Makes 1 cup sauce

Mustard Sauce

¼ cup sugar
½ tablespoon all-purpose flour
2 teaspoons dry mustard
1 egg yolk, beaten
1 cup whipping cream
¼ cup cider vinegar

1. Mix sugar, flour, mustard, egg and ¼ cup of the cream in small saucepan. Cook over low heat, gradually stirring in remaining cream.

2. Cook, stirring constantly, until thick.

3. Stir in vinegar gradually.

Makes 1 cup sauce

Tip:
If your pressure cooker has a variable pressure regulator, you can cook meats at 10 pounds pressure, which is the equivalent of 238°F or 114°C; since meat cooks more slowly than at 15 pounds pressure (250°F or 121°C), it retains slightly more of its juices.

Carbonnades à la Flamande (Beef and Onions Braised in Beer)

Cook under pressure at 10 lbs. for 15 minutes (or at 15 lbs. for 12 minutes).

Carbonnades à la Flamande is Belgium's most famous braise and is quite different from the red wine-flavored French boeuf bourguignon. Dark beer softened with a little brown sugar and a dash of wine vinegar in the gravy provide unusual flavor. This traditional dish calls for more onions than most stews, but does not include vegetables such as potatoes and carrots.

2 pounds boneless, beef round steak
Flour for coating
2 tablespoons vegetable oil
4 cups sliced onions
2 cloves garlic, finely chopped
1 teaspoon salt
¼ teaspoon pepper
1 tablespoon light brown sugar
1½ cups dark beer
Bouquet garni (1 sprig parsley, 1 bay leaf, 1 teaspoon dried thyme leaves tied in a cheesecloth bag)
1 tablespoon cornstarch
1 tablespoon vinegar

1. Wipe meat with damp cloth, paper towel dry. Cut beef into slices 2 x 4 x ½-inch thick. Lightly coat meat in flour. Heat oil in cooker. Cook meat, a few pieces at a time, until brown on all sides. Remove from cooker.

2. Add onions and garlic to cooker; sauté until tender, adding more oil if necessary. Remove from cooker and season with salt and pepper.

3. Place half the meat in the cooker; arrange half the onions over meat. Sprinkle lightly with brown sugar. Repeat with remaining meat and onions; pour in beer. Add bouquet garni. Heat to boiling.

4. Cover and set control at 10. Cook over high heat until pressure is reached. Reduce heat; cook 15 minutes (at 15 pounds pressure, cook 12 minutes).

5. Reduce pressure at once by placing cooker under cold, running water.

6. Remove meat mixture to serving platter; keep warm. Measure 1½ cups cooking liquid into cooker; heat to boiling. Mix cornstarch and vinegar; stir into boiling liquid. Cook, stirring constantly, until liquid thickens. Serve over meat.

Makes 4 to 6 servings

Fruited Pot Roast

Cook under pressure at 10 lbs. for 60 minutes (or at 15 lbs. for 45 minutes).

Dried fruits cooked with the juicy roast create a wonderful fragrant gravy and an attractive way of serving.

3 pounds beef pot roast, rolled and tied
1 tablespoon vegetable oil
1 teaspoon salt
½ teaspoon black pepper
12 dried apricots
12 pitted prunes
1 tablespoon instant minced onion

1. Damp wipe meat and dry with paper towels.

2. Heat oil in cooker. Brown meat on all sides.

3. Remove meat and place in center of heavy-duty foil; sprinkle with salt and pepper. Arrange apricots, prunes and onion around meat; sprinkle with cinnamon and ginger.

4. Bring aluminum foil up around meat, leaving top open. Pour wine over meat.

Fruited Pot Roast (Continued)

1 teaspoon ground cinnamon
1 teaspoon ground ginger
½ cup sweet red wine
2 cups water

5. Add water to cooker; place meat packet on rack in cooker.

6. Cover and set control at 10. Cook over high heat until pressure is reached. Reduce heat; cook 60 minutes (at 15 pounds pressure, cook 45 minutes).

7. Cool cooker naturally 5 minutes; place cooker under cold, running water to complete pressure reduction.

8. Remove roast to serving platter, top with pan juices. Arrange fruits around roast.

Makes 4 to 6 servings

Tip:

You can cook any of your favorite pot roast recipes in the pressure cooker with good results. Use two cups of water, wine or other liquid for a 2 ½ to 3 pound roast; cook 50 to 60 minutes.

Shyrle's Rouladen

Cook under pressure at 10 lbs. for 8 to 10 minutes (or at 15 lbs. for 6 to 8 minutes).

This recipe comes to us all the way from Germany, courtesy of Shyrle Hacker. It makes a great appetizer to serve with cocktails.

2 pounds eye of round beef, cut into 12 thin slices
1 teaspoon salt
¼ teaspoon pepper
1 tablespoon prepared mustard
4 slices bacon, cut into thirds
1 large onion, peeled, thinly sliced
1 large dill pickle, minced
⅔ cup water
2 tablespoons all-purpose flour
¼ cup water
⅛ teaspoon garlic salt
⅛ teaspoon chili powder
⅛ teaspoon Worcestershire sauce
1 tablespoon dry red wine

1. Pound meat slices until very thin; sprinkle with salt and pepper. Rub mustard over each piece.

2. Cook bacon in cooker until light brown; remove from cooker. Cook onion in bacon drippings until limp.

3. Divide bacon, onion and dill pickle over pieces of meat. Turn in ends and roll; fasten each roll with toothpick. Brown meat rolls in drippings in cooker. Add ⅔ cup water.

4. Cover and set control at 10. Cook over high heat until pressure is reached. Reduce heat; cook 8 to 10 minutes (at 15 pounds pressure, cook 6 to 8 minutes).

5. Cool cooker naturally 5 minutes; place cooker under cold, running water to complete pressure reduction.

6. Remove meat rolls to serving platter; keep warm.

7. Heat cooking liquid in cooker. Mix flour and ¼ cup water; stir into liquid in cooker. Stir in garlic salt, chili powder, Worcestershire sauce and red wine. Cook, stirring constantly, until thickened. Serve over meat rolls.

Makes 4 servings of 3 rolls each

Barbecued Short Ribs, Western Style

Marinate meat 4 to 6 hours before cooking.

Cook under pressure at 10 lbs. for 45 minutes (or at 15 lbs. for 30 to 35 minutes).

Marinate and cook beef short ribs in a thick, spicy sauce for a real country taste treat.

2 tablespoons vegetable oil
1 cup catsup
2 tablespoons dry red wine
1 tablespoon Worcestershire sauce
2 drops hot sauce
1 tablespoon prepared mustard
1 tablespoon brown sugar
1 scant teaspoon chili powder
1 teaspoon salt
⅛ teaspoon pepper
3 pounds beef short ribs, cut into serving pieces
2 tablespoons vegetable oil
2 tablespoons finely-chopped onion
1 cup water
Flour (see Preparation)
Water (see Preparation)

1. Mix 2 tablespoons oil, the catsup, wine, Worcestershire sauce, hot sauce, mustard, brown sugar, chili powder, salt and pepper. Brush all sides of ribs with mixture. Cover and let stand 4 to 6 hours.

2. Heat 2 tablespoons oil in cooker and sauté onion until tender.

3. Add ribs; cook until brown on both sides. Pour in 1 cup of water and remaining marinade.

4. Cover and set control at 10. Cook over high heat until pressure is reached. Reduce heat; cook 45 minutes (at 15 pounds pressure, cook 30 to 35 minutes).

5. Cool cooker naturally 5 minutes; place cooker under cold, running water to complete pressure reduction. Remove ribs to a platter; and keep warm.

6. Measure liquid in cooker and return to cooker; heat to boiling. Mix 1 tablespoon flour with ¼ cup cold water for each cup of meat liquid. Stir into cooker; cook, stirring constantly, until mixture thickens. Serve over ribs.

Makes 4 servings

Stuffed Cabbage

Cook under pressure at 15 lbs. for 10 minutes. Include an extra 35 minutes to simmer ingredients. (See recipe how-to on pages 67-68.)

There are many versions of this European favorite, but we especially like this one, which is spiced with caraway seeds and sauced with fresh tomatoes.

1 large cabbage
Boiling water (enough to cover)
1 pound ground beef
1 medium onion, grated
1 small potato, peeled, grated
1 teaspoon caraway seeds
¾ cup cooked rice
½ cup tomato juice
1 teaspoon salt
⅛ teaspoon pepper
⅔ cup beef stock

1. Cut core from head of cabbage; place cabbage in cooker. Cover with boiling water. Cover cooker and let stand until cool. Drain; separate cabbage leaves.

2. Cook ground beef in pressure cooker until brown. Stir in onion, potato, caraway, rice, tomato juice, 1 teaspoon salt and the pepper.

3. Spoon about 2 tablespoons beef mixture onto each cabbage leaf (overlap smaller leaves to make use of entire cabbage, if necessary). Fold in cabbage ends and roll up loosely.

Stuffed Cabbage (Continued)

1 tablespoon oil
3 medium tomatoes, coarsely
    chopped
1 small can (4 ounces) tomato
    sauce
1 tablespoon sugar
½ teaspoon salt

4. Place cabbage rolls, seam-sides-down, on rack in cooker. Add beef stock and 1 tablespoon oil.

5. Cover and set control at 15. Cook over high heat until pressure is reached. Reduce heat; cook 10 minutes.

6. Cool cooker naturally 5 minutes; place cooker under cold, running water to complete pressure reduction. Remove cabbage rolls to platter.

7. Stir tomatoes, tomato sauce, sugar and ½ teaspoon salt into cooking liquid. Simmer uncovered 5 minutes. Place cabbage rolls, seam-sides-down, in sauce. Cover cooker, but do not place control on lid. Simmer over low heat ½ hour.

Makes 6 to 8 servings

Tips:

You can substitute wine, bouillon or stock for part or all of the water specified in meat recipes. Always reduce heat once pressure has been reached.

If your pressure cooker has a variable pressure regulator, you can cook meats at 10 pounds pressure, which is the equivalent of 238°F or 114°C; since meat cooks more slowly than at 15 pounds pressure (250°F or 121°C), it retains slightly more of its juices.

Never fill pressure cooker more than two-thirds or three-fourths full according to manufacturer's recommendation.

Quick Lamb Curry

Cook under pressure at 10 lbs. for 5 minutes (or at 15 lbs. for 3 minutes).
(See recipe how-to on pages 68-69.)

Apples and raisins add a pleasing touch of sweetness to this quick and easy curry dish. Serve it with your favorite chutney and whichever condiments you wish.

1 tablespoon vegetable oil
3 stalks celery, cut into 1-inch
    pieces
¼ cup chopped onion
2 tablespoons all-purpose flour
2 teaspoons curry powder
½ cup beef stock
¼ cup catsup
½ teaspoon salt
2½ cups cubed lamb
2 red apples, cored, cut into
    eighths
½ cup golden raisins
4 cups cooked rice
    Condiments: chopped chutney,
      peanuts, raisins, almonds,
      apples or toasted coconut

1. Heat oil in cooker; sauté celery and onion until tender. Stir in flour and curry powder. Stir in beef stock, catsup and salt. Add the cubed lamb, apples and raisins.

2. Cover and set control at 10. Cook over high heat until pressure is reached. Reduce heat and cook 5 minutes (at 15 pounds pressure, cook 3 minutes).

3. Cool cooker naturally 5 minutes; place cooker under cold, running water to complete pressure reduction.

4. Serve with rice and condiments.

Makes 4 servings

Lamb Chops with Rosemary

Cook under pressure at 10 lbs. for 8 minutes (or at 15 lbs. for 6 minutes).

The special sweetness of shoulder lamb chops combines well with the flavors of rosemary, sliced potato and onion.

4 shoulder lamb chops, ½-inch thick
1 tablespoon vegetable oil
1 chicken bouillon cube
1 cup hot water
4 potatoes, peeled, sliced
1 large onion, sliced
1 teaspoon dried rosemary leaves
1 teaspoon salt
¼ teaspoon white pepper
2 tablespoons butter or margarine

1. Trim fat from chops. Heat oil in cooker; brown chops on both sides.

2. Dissolve bouillon cube in water; pour into cooker. Place 2 chops on rack in cooker. Arrange half the potatoes and onions on chops; sprinkle with half the rosemary, salt and pepper. Repeat layer. Dot top with butter.

3. Cover and set control at 10. Cook over high heat until pressure is reached. Reduce heat; cook 8 minutes (at 15 pounds pressure, cook 6 minutes).

4. Cool cooker naturally 5 minutes; place cooker under cold, running water to complete pressure reduction.

Makes 2 to 4 servings

Lamb in Dill Sauce

Cook under pressure at 10 lbs. for 13 minutes (or at 15 lbs. for 10 minutes).

Lemon and dill flavor the sauce for this Scandinavian favorite, which is often served with boiled potatoes.

2 tablespoons vegetable oil
2 pounds breast of lamb, cut into 2-inch cubes
1 teaspoon salt
¼ teaspoon white pepper
1 bay leaf
3 sprigs fresh dill or 1 teaspoon dried dillweed
1 sprig parsley
2 cups water

1. Heat oil in cooker; brown meat cubes. Sprinkle meat with 1 teaspoon salt and the pepper. Tie the bay leaf, dill and parsley in cheesecloth bag; add to cooker.

2. Cover meat with water and heat to boiling. Cook until liquid is reduced to 1½ cups, skimming foam occasionally.

3. Cover cooker and set control at 10. Cook over high heat until pressure is reached. Reduce heat; cook 13 minutes (at 15 pounds pressure, cook 10 minutes).

4. Cool cooker naturally 5 minutes; place cooker under cold, running water to complete pressure reduction.

5. Remove meat to serving platter; keep warm. Strain liquid from cooker through a fine sieve or cheesecloth; reserve 1¼ cups liquid.

6. Make Dill Sauce.

Lamb in Dill Sauce (Continued)

Dill Sauce

    1 tablespoon butter or
       margarine
    1 tablespoon all-purpose flour
1¼ cups lamb cooking liquid
1½ teaspoons minced fresh dill
       or ¾ teaspoon dried dill-
       weed
    ½ tablespoon white vinegar
    1 teaspoon sugar
    ¼ teaspoon salt
    1 teaspoon lemon juice
    1 egg yolk, beaten
       Dill or parsley sprigs
       Lemon slices

7. Melt butter in cooker; remove from heat and stir in flour. Add cooking liquid all at once, stirring vigorously until smooth. Heat to boiling; cook, stirring until sauce thickens.

8. Add dill, vinegar, sugar, ¼ teaspoon salt and the lemon juice. Stir 2 tablespoons hot sauce into beaten egg yolk; stir gradually back into sauce.

9. Pour sauce over stew; garnish with dill sprigs and lemon slices.

Makes 4 servings

Tip:

Cooking times given in meat recipes can only be approximate, since even meats of the same weight will vary in size and tenderness. You can check meat for doneness before the end of cooking time by reducing pressure as indicated and removing meat. If meat is not done, return it to the cooker, bring cooker back up to pressure and cook longer.

Polynesian Pork

Marinate meat for 4 hours before cooking. (See recipe how-to on pages 69-70.)

Cook under pressure at 15 lbs. for 10 minutes.

Thinly-sliced and well-spiced pork tenderloin, served with orange and pineapple slices, will prove irresistible.

    2 pounds boneless pork
       tenderloin
    2 tablespoons dry sherry
1½ teaspoons salt
    1 tablespoon pineapple juice
    2 tablespoons soy sauce
    ½ teaspoon ground cinnamon
    ¼ teaspoon ground cloves
    2 tablespoons brown sugar
    2 tablespoons vegetable oil
    1 cup water
       Pineapple slices
       Orange slices
       Prepared mustard
       Soy sauce

1. Cut meat into 2 lengthwise strips. Mix sherry, salt, pineapple juice, 2 tablespoons soy sauce, the cinnamon, cloves and brown sugar. Rub marinade over all surfaces of meat. Place meat in shallow glass dish; pour remaining marinade over. Refrigerate at least 4 hours.

2. Remove meat from marinade; drain on paper toweling. Reserve marinade.

3. Heat oil in cooker; cook pork until brown on all sides. Remove meat; place meat on rack in cooker. Add water; brush meat with reserved marinade.

4. Cover and set control at 15. Cook over high heat until pressure is reached. Reduce heat; cook 10 minutes.

5. Reduce pressure at once by placing cooker under cold, running water.

6. Let meat stand 10 minutes before slicing. Cut into thin slices, about ¼ inch thick. Arrange on platter, garnish with pineapple and orange. Serve hot or cold with small bowls of mustard and soy sauce.

Makes 4 servings

Stuffed Pork Chops

Cook under pressure at 10 lbs. for 16 minutes (or at 15 lbs. for 12 minutes). (See recipe how-to on pages 70-71.)

Caraway and rye bread enliven the stuffing for thick, meaty pork chops.

    4 pork chops, 1-inch thick
1½ tablespoons butter or
        margarine
  1 small onion, chopped
  1 garlic clove, minced
  1 cup soft rye bread crumbs
  ½ teaspoon salt
  ½ teaspoon pepper
  ½ teaspoon caraway seeds
  2 tablespoons minced parsley
  1 egg, slightly beaten
  2 tablespoons water
    Salt
    Pepper
    Flour for dredging
  2 tablespoons butter
  1 cup water

1. Have butcher cut pockets in chops. Heat 1½ tablespoons butter in cooker; sauté onion and garlic until golden. Mix onion and garlic with bread crumbs, ½ teaspoon salt, ½ teaspoon pepper, caraway, parsley, egg and 2 tablespoons water.

2. Stuff chops with bread mixture. Close pockets of chops; secure with toothpicks. Sprinkle chops with salt and pepper to taste. Dust with flour, if desired. Brown on both sides in cooker, adding more butter if necessary. Place chops on rack in cooker. Add 1 cup water.

3. Cover and set control at 10. Cook over high heat until pressure is reached. Reduce heat; cook 16 minutes (at 15 pounds pressure, cook about 12 minutes).

4. Cool cooker naturally 5 minutes; place cooker under cold, running water to complete pressure reduction.

Makes 4 servings

Ham and Yams

Cook under pressure at 10 lbs. for 8 minutes (or at 15 lbs. for 6 minutes).

A Madeira wine sauce flatters an old-fashioned dish of ham and yams. Use as many or as few cloves as you wish for spiciness.

1½ pounds ham slice, cut ¾ inch
        thick
    Whole cloves (see
        Preparation)
  1 tablespoon vegetable oil
  2 tablespoons brown sugar
  ¾ cup water
  2 yams, washed and cut in half
  1 tablespoon arrowroot or
        cornstarch
  ¼ cup Madeira wine
  1 tablespoon butter or
        margarine

1. Cut ham slice into 4 pieces. Press several cloves into each piece. Heat oil in cooker; brown ham. Add brown sugar, water and yams.

2. Cover and set control at 10. Cook over high heat until pressure is reached. Reduce heat; cook 8 minutes (at 15 pounds pressure, cook 6 minutes).

3. Cool cooker naturally 5 minutes; place cooker under cold, running water to complete pressure reduction.

4. Remove ham and yams to serving platter; keep warm.

5. Mix arrowroot with wine; stir into liquid in cooker. Cook, stirring constantly, until clear and slightly thickened, about 1 minute. Stir in 1 tablespoon butter to thicken. Spoon sauce over ham.

Makes 4 servings

Meat~Stuffed Green Peppers

Cook under pressure at 10 lbs. for 15 minutes (or at 15 lbs. for 12 minutes).

This familiar combination is always welcome at the dinner table — especially when the traditional filling is varied with brown rice and ham.

4 green peppers
Boiling water (enough to cover)
½ pound ground veal
¼ pound ground cooked ham
½ cup cooked brown rice
1 teaspoon salt
⅛ teaspoon pepper
1 egg
¼ cup milk
1 tablespoon instant minced onion
1 cup tomato juice
1 cup water
2 teaspoons all-purpose flour

1. Slice tops off stem end of peppers; scoop out seeds. Cook peppers in boiling water 3 minutes; drain and cool.

2. Combine meats, rice, salt, pepper, egg, milk, onion and ½ cup tomato juice.

3. Stuff peppers lightly, allowing space for filling to expand. Set tops on peppers. Stand peppers on rack in cooker; add 1 cup water.

4. Cover and set control at 10. Cook over high heat until pressure is reached. Reduce heat; cook 15 minutes (at 15 pounds pressure, cook 12 minutes).

5. Cool cooker naturally 5 minutes; place cooker under cold, running water to complete pressure reduction.

6. Mix remaining ½ cup tomato juice and flour; heat to boiling. Cook, stirring constantly, until thickened. Spoon over peppers.

Makes 4 servings

Glazed Smoked Pork

Cook under pressure at 10 lbs. for 35 minutes (or at 15 lbs. for 25 minutes). Include an extra 30 minutes for baking.

Pressure cooking speeds the preparation of a pork shoulder roast, which is first cooked and then baked with a fruit juice glaze.

1½ pounds smoked pork shoulder
1 cup water
¼ cup pineapple juice
¼ cup orange juice
¼ cup packed brown sugar
1 tablespoon prepared mustard
1½ tablespoons all-purpose flour
¼ cup cold water

1. Place meat on rack in cooker. Add 1 cup water.

2. Cover and set control at 10. Cook over high heat until pressure is reached. Reduce heat; cook 35 minutes (at 15 pounds pressure, cook 25 minutes).

3. Cool cooker naturally 5 minutes; place cooker under cold, running water to complete pressure reduction.

4. Remove meat from cooker; place in baking pan. Mix pineapple and orange juices, brown sugar and mustard; brush over surface of meat. Bake at 325°F for 30 minutes.

5. Place meat on serving platter; keep warm. Heat remaining sauce to boiling; stir in flour mixed with ¼ cup water. Cook, stirring constantly, until thickened. Serve sauce over meat.

Makes 4 servings

Spareribs with Beer

Marinate the meat for 24 hours before cooking.

Cook under pressure at 10 lbs. for 20 minutes (or at 15 lbs. for 15 minutes).

Beer gives these ribs plenty of hearty flavor. Serve them with sauerkraut and boiled potatoes, if you wish.

3 pounds pork spareribs, cut
    into serving pieces
1½ cups beer
½ cup honey
½ teaspoon dry mustard
1 teaspoon chili powder
1 teaspoon lemon juice
1 tablespoon vegetable oil

1. Place ribs in a long baking dish. Mix remaining ingredients except oil and pour over ribs. Refrigerate at least 24 hours, turning occasionally.

2. Remove ribs from dish; reserve marinade. Heat oil in cooker; cook ribs until brown on both sides. Remove ribs; arrange ribs on rack in cooker. Pour reserved marinade over ribs.

3. Cover and set control at 10. Cook over high heat until pressure is reached. Reduce heat; cook 20 minutes (at 15 pounds pressure, cook 15 minutes).

4. Cool cooker naturally 5 minutes; place cooker under cold, running water to complete pressure reduction. (For extra crispness, ribs may be placed on broiler pan and broiled 2 minutes on each side before serving.)

5. Place ribs on serving platter. Simmer cooking juices until thickened to desired consistency; serve over ribs.

Makes 4 servings

Veal Meatballs

Cook under pressure at 10 lbs. for 5 minutes (or at 15 lbs. for 3 to 4 minutes).

Serve these delicious meatballs with your favorite sauce or enjoy them plain with rice or mashed potatoes.

1¼ pounds ground veal
¼ pound ground pork
2 eggs
½ cup cream
2 tablespoons milk
1 tablespoon instant minced
    onion
1 teaspoon salt
¼ teaspoon pepper
    Dash ground nutmeg
3 slices toasted whole wheat
    bread, finely crumbled
3 tablespoons butter or
    margarine
1 cup water

1. Mix veal, pork, eggs, cream, milk, onion, salt, pepper, nutmeg and bread crumbs. Form meat mixture into 1-inch balls.

2. Heat butter in cooker. Cook meatballs until brown. Remove meatballs; place on rack in cooker. Add water.

3. Cover and set control at 10. Cook over high heat until pressure is reached. Reduce heat; cook 5 minutes (at 15 pounds pressure, cook 3 to 4 minutes).

4. Cool cooker naturally 5 minutes; place cooker under cold, running water to complete pressure reduction.

Makes 4 servings

Veal with Caraway

Marinate the meat for 4 hours before cooking.

Cook under pressure at 10 lbs. for 45 minutes (or at 15 lbs. for 35 minutes).

This savory roast of veal, served with a flavorful sour cream and caper sauce, is bound to please friends and family.

2 cloves, crushed
¼ teaspoon caraway seeds
4 tablespoons butter or
   margarine
3 to 3½ pounds boneless
   veal rump
2 cups dry white wine
   Water (see Preparation)
1½ tablespoons cornstarch
¼ cup water
½ cup sour cream
2 tablespoons drained capers
1 teaspoon salt
¼ teaspoon pepper

1. Mix cloves, caraway, and 2 tablespoons of the butter into a smooth paste; spread over meat. Roll meat tightly and tie in several places with string.

2. Place meat in a large bowl and add wine; refrigerate at least 4 hours, turning meat twice.

3. Remove meat; reserve marinade. Heat remaining 2 tablespoons butter in cooker; cook meat until brown on all sides. Remove meat; place meat on rack in cooker. Add water to marinade, if necessary, to make two cups. Add marinade to cooker.

4. Cover and set control at 10. Cook over high heat until pressure is reached. Reduce heat; cook 45 minutes (at 15 pounds pressure, cook 35 minutes).

5. Cool cooker naturally 5 minutes; place cooker under cold, running water to complete pressure reduction.

6. Mix cornstarch and ¼ cup water in small saucepan. Stir in 1 cup cooking liquid. Heat to boiling; turn heat to low. Stir in sour cream, capers, salt and pepper. Cook 2 to 3 minutes; do not boil. Serve with veal.

Makes 6 to 8 servings

Tips:

Always check the vent tube by holding the cover up to the light before using your pressure cooker; light should be visible through the tube.

Cooking times given in meat recipes can only be approximate, since even meats of the same weight will vary in size and tenderness. You can check meat for doneness before the end of cooking time by reducing pressure as indicated and removing meat. If meat is not done, return it to the cooker, bring cooker back up to pressure and cook longer.

Wine-Sauced Veal

Cook under pressure at 10 lbs. for 6 to 8 minutes (or at 15 lbs. for 5 to 6 minutes).

A robust sauce beautifully complements the flavor of veal steaks or chops. And pressure cooking makes the meat juicy and tender.

1½ pounds veal round steaks or veal chops
¼ cup all-purpose flour
1 teaspoon salt
½ teaspoon pepper
2 tablespoons vegetable oil
¼ cup chopped onion
1 garlic clove, minced
½ cup water
½ cup dry red wine
1 cup tomato juice
½ teaspoon dried rosemary leaves
½ teaspoon dried basil leaves
¼ cup minced parsley

1. Coat veal with mixture of flour, salt and pepper.
2. Heat oil in cooker; brown meat on all sides. Remove meat.
3. Add onion and garlic; sauté until onion is tender. Add remaining ingredients; heat to boiling. Place meat on rack in cooker.
4. Cover and set control at 10. Cook over high heat until pressure is reached. Reduce heat; cook 6 to 8 minutes (at 15 pounds pressure, cook 5 to 6 minutes).
5. Cool cooker naturally 5 minutes; place cooker under cold, running water to complete pressure reduction.
6. Spoon some of the cooking liquid over veal to serve.

Makes 4 servings

Veal Roll-Ups

Cook under pressure at 10 lbs. for 4 minutes (or at 15 lbs. for 3 minutes).

A treat for anyone who loves anchovies, this recipe wraps them with cheese in thin slices of veal. Marsalla wine accents the sauce.

1½ pounds veal round, cut into ¼-inch slices
¼ pound sliced mozzarella cheese
6 to 8 anchovy fillets, drained
2 tablespoons butter or margarine
½ can (10½-ounce size) beef bouillon
½ cup water
1 tablespoon Marsalla wine
2 tablespoons butter or margarine
1 teaspoon minced parsley

1. Pound veal slices until very thin. Divide cheese on meat slices; place an anchovy fillet on each. Roll meat slices; secure with toothpicks.
2. Heat 2 tablespoons butter in cooker; cook veal rolls until brown on all sides. Remove rolls; place on rack, seam-sides-down, in cooker. Pour in bouillon and water.
3. Cover and set control at 10. Cook over high heat until pressure is reached. Reduce heat; cook 4 minutes (at 15 pounds pressure, cook 3 minutes).
4. Cool cooker naturally 5 minutes; place cooker under cold, running water to complete pressure reduction.
5. Place rolls on serving platter. Heat liquid in cooker to boiling; cook until reduced by one third. Reduce heat; add wine and 2 tablespoons butter. Cook and stir over medium heat until butter is melted. Add the parsley. Pour sauce over rolls.

Makes 4 servings

Chicken

THE PRESSURE cooker works such wonders with chicken that we've developed a whole world of recipes around this single ingredient. Dishes range from French-style Chicken Burgundy and Chicken Marengo to South Seas Chicken, Basque-style Paella and Italian-Style Chicken Saltimbocca. Pressure cooking makes chicken juicier and the steam infuses it with the fragrance of accompanying seasonings.

In every recipe, we maximize flavor and appearance by browning the cut-up chicken in butter or vegetable oil in the open cooker before pressure cooking. But there similarities end and various methods of seasoning and saucing take over. For Stewed Chicken with Potatoes and Dumplings, for example, we spice the chicken with a touch of nutmeg and cook it with potatoes in white wine; steam dumplings in the cooking liquid; and then make a creamy mushroom gravy for the chicken and potatoes. Buttermilk Chicken is coated with crushed seasoned poultry stuffing and cooked in buttermilk. Peanut Drumsticks are marinated, cooked, and then rolled in crushed peanuts — they make unusually good cocktail-hour fare.

Cooking Liquid

In some recipes, the chicken is poached directly in the cooking liquid; in others, it is steamed on the rack. The liquid in which the chicken is poached influences flavor a great deal; so we almost always use red or white wine, buttermilk, sour cream or yogurt thinned with water or wine, or fruit juice. The only exception to this rule is Red Chicken, which is spiced strongly enough with curry powder, cumin and saffron not to need additional flavoring. In all such recipes, the cooking liquid becomes an excellent gravy or sauce with the addition of flour or cornstarch to thicken it and last-minute touches like cognac or sherry.

Whether the chicken is poached or steamed, it sometimes requires a few minutes of crisping under the broiler after it has been pressure cooked. This combination of pressure cooking and broiling produces dishes like Deviled Chicken and Peanut Drumsticks that are more moist and flavorful than conventionally-broiled chicken, since broiling not only tends to dry out the food but also limits the absorption of seasonings.

The treasury of ingredients in Basque-Style Paella results in a glorious one-pot meal of sausage, chicken, shrimp, clams and artichokes. As with all paellas, rice tinted golden with saffron or turmeric binds the colorful melange. The Paella needs only 1 minute of cooking under pressure and when you open the cooker, you'll see that much of the cooking liquid has not been absorbed. If you let the cooker stand, uncovered, the rice will finish cooking in the heat that remains in the pot and the liquid will be absorbed in about five minutes.

Cooking Times

None of the recipes in this chapter require more than 15 minutes of pressure cooking. When appropriate, we have given cooking times at both 10 and 15 pounds pressure so that you can use whichever you prefer. Cooking times are so short that the difference in temperature produces very little difference in the texture of the finished food. You can cook chicken that's only partially thawed in the pressure cooker, but you may have to increase cooking times by one minute. If you want to adapt your own chicken recipes to pressure cooking, use the same amounts of chicken and cooking liquid and follow the same cooking time and method of reducing pressure specified in a similar recipe.

Stewed Chicken with Potatoes and Dumplings

Cook under pressure at 15 lbs. for 10 minutes. Include an extra 10 minutes to simmer dumplings.

This hearty dish never goes out of style. Steam the herbed Dumplings in the cooking liquid before you prepare the sauce.

1½ tablespoons all-purpose flour
1 teaspoon salt
⅛ teaspoon white pepper
⅛ teaspoon ground nutmeg
2½ to 3 pound chicken, cut into serving pieces
2 tablespoons vegetable oil, or more if needed
1 garlic clove, minced
4 medium potatoes, pared
½ cup water
½ cup dry white wine
Dumplings (recipe follows)
2 tablespoons butter or margarine
2 tablespoons all-purpose flour
1 cup chicken stock
½ cup cream
1 egg yolk
1 tablespoon lemon juice
1 can (4 ounces) sliced mushrooms, undrained
Paprika

1. Mix flour, salt, pepper, and nutmeg; coat chicken pieces with mixture.

2. Heat oil in cooker; cook chicken and garlic until light brown.

3. Add potatoes, water and wine.

4. Cover and set control at 15. Cook over moderate heat until pressure is reached. Reduce heat; cook 10 minutes.

5. Reduce pressure at once by placing cooker under cold, running water.

6. Remove potatoes to serving platter; keep warm.

7. Make Dumplings (recipe follows).

8. Heat butter in cooker; stir in flour to make smooth paste. Remove from heat. Stir in stock and cream gradually.

9. Heat to boiling, stirring constantly.

10. Beat egg yolk and lemon juice; stir gradually into cooker. Cook, stirring constantly, until mixture thickens. Stir in mushrooms, adding enough mushroom liquid for desired consistency. Cut potatoes into quarters and spoon gravy over chicken, potatoes and dumplings. Sprinkle with paprika.

Makes 4 servings

Dumplings

1½ cups all-purpose flour
2 teaspoons baking powder
½ teaspoon dried sweet basil leaves
½ teaspoon dried thyme leaves
1 teaspoon salt
1 egg
½ cup milk

1. Mix flour, baking powder, herbs and salt in medium bowl; stir in egg and milk.

2. Drop batter from spoon over chicken and liquid in cooker. Simmer, uncovered, 5 minutes.

3. Cover cooker; cook 5 minutes without control on vent. Remove chicken and dumplings to serving platter. Discard cooking liquid.

Tip:
Always check the vent tube by holding the cover up to the light before using pressure cooker; light should be visible through the tube.

Chicken Marengo

Cook under pressure at 10 lbs. for 10 minutes (or at 15 lbs. for 8 minutes).

This is a classic medley that adapts well to pressure cooking. Onion, garlic, white wine, olives and cognac enhance the combination of chicken and vegetables.

3 tablespoons olive or vegetable oil
1 onion, sliced
2½ to 3 pound chicken, quartered
1 clove garlic, minced
½ pound fresh mushrooms, sliced
10 small boiling onions, peeled
1 cup dry white wine
1 can (16 ounces) Italian-style tomatoes, undrained
1 can (3½ ounces) pitted ripe olives, drained
1 ounce cognac

1. Heat oil in cooker; sauté sliced onion until tender and remove. Cook chicken and garlic in oil until chicken is light brown; remove. Cook mushrooms and boiling onions 2 minutes. Stir in ½ cup of the wine, the tomatoes, chicken, garlic and sliced onion.

2. Cover and set control at 10. Cook over moderate heat until pressure is reached. Reduce heat; cook 10 minutes (at 15 pounds pressure, cook 8 minutes).

3. Cool cooker naturally 5 minutes; place under cold, running water to complete pressure reduction.

4. Arrange chicken on platter; keep warm. Add remaining wine, the olives and cognac to cooker. Simmer, uncovered, until hot and of desired consistency. Pour sauce over chicken.

Makes 4 servings

Deviled Chicken

Cook under pressure at 10 lbs. for 10 to 12 minutes (or at 15 lbs. for 8 to 9 minutes).

Dijon-style mustard and vinegar give this chicken an excitingly different flavor. Serve it with rice and fresh string beans.

2 tablespoons butter or margarine
1 teaspoon salt
1 teaspoon cider vinegar
½ teaspoon paprika
½ teaspoon Dijon-style mustard
1¾ pound chicken, split in half
½ cup dry white wine
½ cup water
½ cup soft breadcrumbs
2 tablespoons butter or margarine, melted

1. Mix 2 tablespoons butter, the salt, vinegar, paprika and mustard. Spread mixture over all sides of the chicken.

2. Cook chicken over medium heat in cooker until golden on all sides. Remove chicken; place on rack in cooker. Pour in wine and water. Mix bread crumbs and melted butter; sprinkle over chicken.

3. Cover and set control at 10. Cook over moderate heat until pressure is reached. Reduce heat; cook 10 to 12 minutes (at 15 pounds pressure, cook 8 to 9 minutes).

4. Cool cooker naturally 5 minutes; place cooker under cold, running water to complete pressure reduction.

5. Place chicken in baking dish; broil until bread crumbs are crisp, about 2 minutes.

Makes 2 servings

Chicken Saltimbocca

Cook under pressure at 15 lbs. for 5 minutes.

The term "saltimbocca" is derived from the Italian phrase for "pop in your mouth." Taste this dish and you'll understand how it got its name!

- 2 large chicken breasts, skinned, boned, cut into halves
- 8 paper-thin slices prosciutto or pressed cooked ham
- 4 slices mozzarella or Swiss cheese
- 1 tomato, chopped
- ½ teaspoon dried savory leaves
- ½ teaspoon dried basil leaves
- ½ cup Italian-style bread crumbs
- ⅓ cup grated Parmesan cheese
- 2 tablespoons minced parsley
- ¼ cup butter or margarine
- 1 cup dry vermouth

1. Place chicken, boned side up, on cutting board; cover with plastic wrap. Pound lightly with smooth side of meat mallet, until ¼ inch thick, being careful to keep the chicken intact.
2. Place 2 ham slices and 1 cheese slice on each chicken piece; divide tomato on each and sprinkle with savory and basil.
3. Roll chicken, tucking in sides; secure with toothpicks. Mix bread crumbs, Parmesan and parsley in bowl; coat chicken rolls with mixture.
4. Heat butter in cooker; sauté chicken until golden. Add vermouth.
5. Cover and set control at 15. Cook over moderate heat until pressure is reached. Reduce heat; cook 5 minutes.
6. Reduce pressure at once by placing cooker under cold, running water.

Makes 4 servings

Tip:
You can substitute wine, bouillon or stock for part or all of water specified in chicken recipes. Always reduce heat once pressure has been reached.

Chicken in Cream Sauce

Cook under pressure at 15 lbs. for 8 minutes.

Delicate seasonings and a rich sauce combine to make this chicken specialty a truly elegant delight for all.

- 2 to 3 pound chicken, cut into serving pieces
- 1 teaspoon salt
- ⅛ teaspoon white pepper
- 3 tablespoons butter or margarine
- 2 tablespoons chopped onion
- 1 teaspoon finely-chopped chives
- ½ teaspoon dried tarragon leaves
- 1 teaspoon minced parsley
- ¾ cup water
- ¼ cup Madeira wine

1. Wipe chicken pieces with a damp cloth and pat dry with paper towels. Sprinkle chicken with 1 teaspoon salt and ⅛ teaspoon pepper. Heat 3 tablespoons butter in cooker; cook chicken until light brown on all sides. Add onion, chives, tarragon and parsley.
2. Place rack in cooker; pour in water. Place chicken on rack and spoon Madeira wine over chicken.
3. Cover and set control at 15. Cook over moderate heat until pressure is reached. Reduce heat; cook 8 minutes.
4. Cool cooker naturally 5 minutes; place cooker under cold, running water to complete pressure reduction.

Chicken in Cream Sauce (Continued)

2 tablespoons butter or
    margarine
1 tablespoon all-purpose flour
1 cup warm milk
½ cup whipping cream or half-
    and-half
¼ teaspoon salt
⅛ teaspoon cayenne pepper
2 egg yolks, beaten
⅛ teaspoon paprika
6 whole mushrooms, cut into
    slices
    Parsley

5. Arrange chicken on platter; keep warm. Reserve ½ cup cooking liquid.

6. Make Cream Sauce.

7. Heat 2 tablespoons butter in cooker. Stir in flour to make smooth paste. Remove from heat; gradually stir in milk and cream. Stir in ¼ teaspoon salt and the cayenne. Cook, stirring constantly, until mixture boils. Reduce heat to low.

8. Stir ¼ cup sauce slowly into yolks. Stir egg mixture into thickened milk mixture in cooker. Stir in paprika.

9. Stir ½ cup reserved cooking liquid into sauce. Stir in mushrooms and simmer two minutes. Pour sauce over chicken; garnish with parsley.

Makes 4 servings

Tip:
Always check the vent tube by holding the cover up to the light before using pressure cooker; light should be visible through the tube.

Basque-Style Paella

Cook under pressure at 15 lbs. for 1 minute.

Enjoy this flavorful one-pot entrée with crusty French bread, fresh peas and glasses of dry white table wine.

1 tablespoon vegetable oil
¾ pound mild chorizos
    (Mexican sausages),
    casings removed
6 green onions, sliced
1 medium onion, chopped
1 large clove garlic, minced
1 whole chicken breast,
    skinned, boned, cut into 1-
    inch pieces
2 tablespoons vegetable oil
1 cup uncooked rice
⅛ teaspoon saffron or ground
    turmeric
2 cups chicken broth
2 teaspoons lemon juice
½ pound raw shrimp, shelled
    and deveined
1 tablespoon chopped pimiento
1 jar (4 ounces) marinated
    artichoke hearts, drained
8 ounces fresh or canned
    chopped clams with juice
    Lemon wedges

1. Heat 1 tablespoon oil in cooker; cook sausage until brown; remove sausage and drain all but 2 tablespoons dripping. Heat drippings in cooker; sauté green onions, onion, and garlic until onions are tender. Stir in chicken, cooking until chicken turns white. Remove mixture from cooker; reserve.

2. Heat 2 tablespoons oil in cooker; cook rice and saffron, stirring occasionally, until rice is light brown. Stir in chicken broth and lemon juice. Heat to boiling.

3. Stir in sausage and chicken. Add shrimp. Sprinkle with pimiento. Add artichoke hearts and clams.

4. Cover and set control at 15. Cook over high heat until pressure is reached. Cook 1 minute.

5. Cool cooker naturally 5 minutes; place cooker under cold, running water to complete pressure reduction.

6. Fluff rice with fork; let stand, uncovered, until liquid is fully absorbed and rice is done, about 5 minutes. Garnish with lemon wedges.

Makes 4 servings

Chicken in Raisin Sauce

Cook under pressure at 15 lbs. for 8 minutes.

Blend sour cream and golden raisins into an unusual delicately sweet sauce. Serve the chicken and creamy sauce over rice or noodles.

2 tablespoons butter or
   margarine
1 cup coarsely-chopped onions
2½ to 3 pound chicken, cut into
   serving pieces
1 cup sour cream or yogurt
1 cup golden raisins
½ cup dry white wine
1 tablespoon cornstarch
¼ cup water
4 cups cooked rice or noodles

1. Heat 1 tablespoon of the butter in cooker; sauté onions until light brown. Remove; reserve.

2. Brush chicken pieces on all sides with half the sour cream. Heat remaining butter in cooker; cook chicken until golden on all sides. Add remaining sour cream, sautéed onions, raisins and wine.

3. Cover and set control at 15. Cook over high heat until pressure is reached. Reduce heat; cook 8 minutes.

4. Reduce pressure at once by placing cooker under cold, running water.

5. Remove chicken and arrange on platter. Mix cornstarch and water; stir into cooker. Cook over medium heat, stirring constantly, until thickened.

6. Place chicken in cooker; simmer until hot, about 5 minutes. Serve chicken over rice or noodles.

Makes 4 servings

Yogurt Chicken

Cook under pressure at 10 lbs. for 6 to 8 minutes (or at 15 lbs. for 5 to 6 minutes).

Water chestnuts add a delightful crunch to this nutritious dish. Thyme and tarragon create a wonderful aroma as the chicken cooks.

2 whole chicken breasts, boned,
   cut into halves
¼ cup all-purpose flour
1 teaspoon salt
¼ teaspoon white pepper
¼ teaspoon dried thyme leaves
⅛ teaspoon dried tarragon
   leaves
¼ cup butter or margarine
1 cup water
   Paprika
1 cup plain yogurt
½ cup sliced water chestnuts

1. Wipe chicken breasts with a damp cloth and pat dry with paper towels. Coat chicken with mixture of flour, salt, pepper, thyme and tarragon.

2. Heat butter in cooker; cook chicken until golden. Remove chicken; place on rack in cooker. Add water; sprinkle chicken lightly with paprika.

3. Cover and set control at 10. Cook over moderate heat until pressure is reached. Reduce heat; cook 6 to 8 minutes (at 15 pounds pressure, cook 5 to 6 minutes).

4. Cool cooker naturally 5 minutes; place cooker under cold, running water to complete pressure reduction.

5. Arrange chicken on platter; keep warm. Remove all but ¼ cup cooking liquid from cooker. Stir yogurt and water chestnuts into liquid in cooker; cook over low heat until of desired consistency. Serve over chicken.

Makes 4 servings

Peanut Drumsticks

Marinate chicken at least 6 hours before cooking.

Cook under pressure at 10 lbs. for 6 minutes (or at 15 lbs. for 4 minutes).

The novel crushed peanut coating makes these drumsticks a terrific cocktail hour appetizer. Substitute chicken wings, if you prefer these for "finger food."

8 chicken drumsticks or wings
½ cup orange juice
1 tablespoon catsup
1 tablespoon soy sauce
½ teaspoon Worcestershire sauce
2 tablespoons vegetable oil
1 tablespoon lemon juice
½ teaspoon salt
2 tablespoons butter or margarine
1 cup water
⅓ cup finely-ground peanuts

1. Wipe drumsticks with a damp cloth and pat dry with paper towels. Set aside. Mix all ingredients except butter, water, and peanuts; coat chicken with mixture. Refrigerate 6 hours or overnight; drain, reserving marinade.

2. Heat butter in cooker; cook chicken until light brown. Remove chicken; place on rack in cooker. Add water to cooker. Brush chicken with remaining marinade.

3. Cover and set control at 10. Cook over moderate heat until pressure is reached. Reduce heat; cook 6 minutes (at 15 pounds pressure, cook 4 minutes).

4. Cool cooker naturally 5 minutes; place cooker under cold, running water to complete pressure reduction.

5. Roll each drumstick in peanuts. Arrange on a baking sheet, place under broiler until brown and crisp; about 2 minutes on each side. Serve hot or cold.

Makes 4 servings

Red Chicken

Cook under pressure at 10 lbs. for 10 minutes (or at 15 lbs. for 8 minutes).

Pretty as a sunset, this colorful chicken dish was inspired by the cuisines of Thailand, India and Pakistan.

2½ pound chicken, cut into serving pieces
2 tablespoons vegetable oil, or more if needed
2 teaspoons curry powder
1½ teaspoons salt
½ teaspoon ground cumin
⅛ teaspoon saffron or ground turmeric
1 onion, finely chopped
1½ teaspoons cider vinegar
1 cup water
2 tablespoons cornstarch
¼ cup water
½ can (4-ounce size) water chestnuts, finely sliced

1. Wipe chicken pieces with a damp cloth and pat dry with paper towels. Heat oil in cooker; cook chicken until crisp and golden on all sides. Sprinkle all sides with mixture of curry, salt, cumin and saffron. Add onion, vinegar and 1 cup water.

2. Cover and set control at 10. Cook over high heat until pressure is reached. Reduce heat; cook 10 minutes (at 15 pounds pressure, cook 8 minutes).

3. Reduce pressure at once by placing cooker under cold, running water.

4. Arrange chicken on platter; keep warm. Heat liquid in cooker to boiling.

5. Mix cornstarch and ¼ cup water; stir into cooker. Cook, stirring constantly, until thickened. Add water chestnuts; cook 1 minute. Spoon sauce over chicken.

Makes 4 servings

Chicken-Avocado Supreme

Cook under pressure at 15 lbs. for 5 to 6 minutes. (See recipe how-to on pages 72- 73.)

The bright colors of avocados, tomatoes and olives add real festivity to this tempting dish. Sprinkle the chicken with cheese and broil briefly just before serving.

2 whole chicken breasts (about 1½ pounds), boned, skinned and cut into halves
1 tablespoon vegetable oil
1 teaspoon salt
1 cup water
8 avocado slices
6 ripe olives, pitted, sliced
4 tomato wedges
¼ cup shredded Cheddar cheese

1. Wipe chicken breast halves with damp cloth and pat dry with paper towels. Heat oil in cooker; cook chicken until brown on both sides. Place chicken on rack in cooker; sprinkle with salt. Add water.

2. Cover and set control at 15. Cook over high heat until pressure is reached. Reduce heat; cook 5 to 6 minutes.

3. Reduce pressure at once by placing cooker under cold, running water.

4. Place each halved chicken breast on 9-inch square of aluminum foil. Bring foil up to form packets, leaving tops open. Place 2 slices of avocado on top of chicken in each packet. Arrange olives on top of each; place a tomato wedge across opening.

5. Cover and set control at 15. Cook over high heat until pressure is reached. Reduce pressure at once by placing cooker under cold, running water.

6. Arrange chicken on oven-proof platter. Sprinkle chicken with cheese. Place under broiler until cheese melts.

Makes 4 servings

Chicken Burgundy

Cook under pressure at 15 lbs. for 8 minutes.

For a rich, robust flavor use a full-bodied Burgundy wine in this popular French classic that is especially good accompanied by parslied potatoes and fresh, green peas.

1 tablespoon butter or margarine
¼ pound ham, cut into ¼ inch pieces
2½ to 3 pound chicken, cut into serving pieces
½ cup all-purpose flour
2 tablespoons butter or margarine
½ teaspoon salt
⅛ teaspoon white pepper
8 small boiling onions, peeled
1 clove garlic, minced
¼ teaspoon dried thyme leaves
1 small bay leaf

1. Heat 1 tablespoon butter in cooker; sauté ham until golden. Remove ham; reserve.

2. Coat chicken with flour. Heat 2 tablespoons butter in cooker; cook chicken until brown on all sides. Sprinkle with salt and pepper. Add reserved ham, onions, garlic, thyme, bay leaf and mushrooms. Pour in wine and chicken stock.

3. Cover and set control at 15. Cook over moderate heat until pressure is reached. Reduce heat; cook 8 minutes.

4. Cool cooker naturally 5 minutes; place cooker under cold, running water to complete pressure reduction.

Chicken Burgundy (Continued)

½ pound fresh mushrooms,
   thinly sliced
1 cup Burgundy wine
½ cup chicken stock
2 tablespoons butter or
   margarine
3 tablespoons all-purpose flour
¼ cup cognac, if desired
   Parsley

5. Arrange chicken mixture in shallow serving bowl, reserving 1¼ cups cooking liquid.

6. Heat 2 tablespoons butter in cooker; stir in flour to make smooth paste. Remove from heat; gradually stir in reserved liquid. Cook, stirring constantly, until gravy thickens.

7. Heat cognac in small saucepan; ignite. Pour flaming cognac into gravy. Serve gravy over chicken. Garnish with parsley.

Makes 4 servings

Tips:

Place chicken under broiler for a few minutes to brown, if desired, after it has been cooked.

You can adapt your own favorite chicken recipe to the pressure cooker by using the same amounts of chicken and cooking liquid and following the same cooking time and method of reducing pressure specified in a similar pressure cooker recipe.

You can substitute wine, bouillon or stock for part or all of water specified in chicken recipes.

South Seas Chicken

Cook under pressure at 10 lbs. for 10 minutes (or at 15 lbs. for 8 minutes). (See recipe how-to on pages 71-72.)

Tropical fruits and juices give this chicken mèlange a flavor reminiscent of the South Seas and the Hawaiian Islands. It invites steamed rice and soy sauce as accompaniments.

¼ cup vegetable oil
4 whole chicken breasts,
   skinned, boned, cut into ½-
   inch strips
½ teaspoon salt
¼ teaspoon white pepper
⅛ teaspoon ground nutmeg
⅛ teaspoon ground cloves
½ cup water
1 can (6 ounces) orange juice
   concentrate
1 can (6 ounces) pineapple
   juice concentrate
1½ tablespoons arrowroot
¼ cup water
½ cup drained pineapple tidbits
¾ cup drained mandarin
   oranges
½ cup blanched slivered
   almonds
2 tablespoons sherry
   Soy sauce

1. Heat oil in pressure cooker; sauté chicken on all sides. Sprinkle chicken with salt, pepper, nutmeg and cloves. Remove chicken and drain liquid from cooker.

2. Place chicken on rack in cooker. Pour in ½ cup water; spoon concentrates over chicken pieces.

3. Cover and set control at 10. Cook over high heat until pressure is reached. Reduce heat; cook 10 minutes (at 15 pounds pressure, cook 8 minutes).

4. Reduce pressure at once by placing cooker under cold, running water.

5. Arrange chicken on platter. Reserve 1 cup of cooking liquid. Place 1 cup liquid in cooker and heat to boiling. Mix arrowroot in ¼ cup water. Stir into cooker. Cook, stirring constantly, until thickened.

6. Stir in pineapple, oranges and almonds; cook 2 minutes over low heat. Stir in sherry. Serve sauce over chicken. Pass the soy sauce.

Makes 4 to 6 servings

Buttermilk Chicken

Cook under pressure at 10 lbs. for 10 minutes (or at 15 lbs. for 8 minutes).

Buttermilk produces an unusually rich and delicious gravy for this easy-to-prepare, country-style chicken dish.

2½ pound chicken, cut into serving pieces
1½ cups buttermilk
1 cup seasoned poultry stuffing mix, crushed
¼ cup minced parsley
½ teaspoon salt
1 teaspoon paprika
2 tablespoons vegetable oil or more, if needed

1. Remove skin from chicken pieces; discard.
2. Rinse chicken and pat dry with paper towels. Dip chicken pieces in buttermilk; reserve remaining buttermilk. Coat chicken with mixture of stuffing mix, parsley, salt and paprika.
3. Heat oil in cooker; cook chicken until light brown on all sides. Remove chicken.
4. Add remaining buttermilk to cooker. Return chicken to cooker.
5. Cover and set control at 10. Heat over high heat until pressure is reached. Reduce heat; cook 10 minutes (at 15 pounds pressure, cook 8 minutes).
6. Cool cooker naturally 5 minutes; place cooker under cold, running water to complete pressure reduction.
7. Place chicken in baking pan; place under broiler until golden. Serve cooking liquid over chicken.
Makes 4 servings

Chicken Fricassee

Cook under pressure at 10 lbs. for 12 minutes (or at 15 lbs. for 10 minutes).

Rice or noodles are the perfect accompaniment for this aromatic fricassee, flavored with ginger and apple juice.

3 pound chicken, cut into serving pieces
1 teaspoon salt
⅛ teaspoon poultry seasoning
⅛ teaspoon white pepper
2 tablespoons vegetable oil
4 pieces crystallized ginger, finely chopped
1 cup warm apple juice
2 tablespoons cornstarch
¼ cup water

1. Wipe chicken pieces with a damp cloth and pat dry with paper towels. Sprinkle chicken with salt, poultry seasoning and pepper. Heat oil in cooker; cook chicken 2 minutes on each side.
2. Place chicken on rack in cooker. Add ginger and apple juice.
3. Cover and set control at 10. Cook over high heat until pressure is reached. Reduce heat; cook 12 minutes (at 15 pounds pressure, cook 10 minutes).
4. Cool cooker naturally 5 minutes; place cooker under cold, running water to complete pressure reduction.
5. Arrange chicken pieces on platter. Strain cooking liquid and add 1 cup to cooker; heat to boiling. Mix cornstarch and water; stir into cooker. Cook, stirring constantly, until thickened.
6. Place chicken in cooker; simmer in sauce until hot, about 5 minutes. *Makes 4 servings*

Seafood

TODAY, WHEN MANY people are seeking both the nutritional benefits of foods low in calories and saturated fats, as well as the convenience of fast food preparation, pressure-cooked fish should prove most welcome.

Most fish recipes cook in less than five minutes and the fish comes out moist and delicately flaky. When you fry, broil or bake fish conventionally, you usually have to use some kind of fat or oil to keep it from drying out, but with pressure cooking, this is not so. You can embellish the fish with a rich sauce after cooking, but you don't have to—a sprinkling of herbs and lemon juice is quite delicious too.

Timing And Freshness

There are two facts you should always remember about pressure cooking fish. First, timing is critical because fish cooks so quickly. The time required is directly related to the thickness of the fish—whether it's whole, filleted or cut into steaks. Play it safe: If the fish you're cooking seems thin for its weight or if it weighs less than a recipe specifies, cook it a shorter amount of time. If you discover, after reducing pressure, that it's not done, you can always bring it back up to pressure and cook it a minute longer.

The second fact to keep in mind is that pressure cooking intensifies the natural flavor and aroma of food. This means that you should never try to pressure cook fish that seems dry or that has a strong, fishy odor. You should cook fresh fish as soon as possible and thawed frozen fish immediately. Allow frozen fish to thaw slowly in the refrigerator, never at room temperature; it needn't be completely thawed before cooking, but it should be sufficiently defrosted for you to handle it easily.

Substituting One Fish For Another

To take advantage of fish in season or supermarket sales, you may want to substitute one kind of fish for another in the recipes. You may do so in most cases as long as the fish is of the same cut, weight and thickness. The simplest substitution is one firm-fleshed fillet for another—flounder, whitefish or ocean perch instead of sole, for example. You may want to try pressure steaming another whole dressed fish in the Stuffed Striped Bass recipe. Some recipes, such as the elegant Salmon Wellington with Lemon Sauce or the Chinese-Steamed Smelts, do not invite substitutions because the fish specified has a distinctive flavor and texture.

Cooking Liquid And Techniques

"Steam-poaching" is the basic technique used with fish: The fish is placed on the rack and allowed to cook in the fragrant steam from the cooking liquid. White wine and fish go especially well together; so we most commonly use wine for all or part of the cooking liquid. Some recipes are enhanced by fish stock or clam juice as the cooking liquid; others by soy sauce, or sherry. When a recipe calls for water as part of the cooking liquid, it's usually because other seasonings are strong enough to provide flavor. You can always substitute fish stock, clam juice or wine for the water.

You'll notice some variations in steam-poaching techniques. Sometimes the recipes call for the fish to be wrapped in foil packets to hold a sauce or stuffing. In these recipes, it's easier to add the cooking liquid before you place the packets on the rack. These dishes take a little longer to cook because the foil slows down heat conduction. Some recipes require that you wrap the fish in cheesecloth; the cheesecloth holds the fish intact and makes it easier to handle. Rolling fillets and securing them with toothpicks serves the same purpose.

Once you get used to the quick timing, you'll come to rely on the pressure cooker for fish perfectly-cooked in many different ways. For the fish recipes, as with meat and chicken, we provide cooking times at both 10 and 15 pounds pressure, so that you can use whichever you prefer.

Salmon Wellington with Lemon Sauce

Cook under pressure at 10 lbs. for 5 minutes (or at 15 lbs. for 3¹/₂ minutes). Include an extra 10 to 12 minutes for baking fish packets.

This superb delicacy lends itself well to modern entertaining for it doesn't take long to prepare. The Lemon Sauce adds to its zestfulness.

4 salmon steaks, ¾ inch thick
1½ teaspoons salt
⅛ teaspoon white pepper
⅛ teaspoon dried dillweed
1 tablespoon instant minced onion
1 tablespoon chopped parsley
¾ cup water
4 frozen puff pastry shells, thawed
1 egg white
1 tablespoon water

Lemon Sauce

⅓ cup butter or margarine
3 tablespoons all-purpose flour
1¼ cups fish stock or clam juice
½ teaspoon salt
⅛ teaspoon white pepper
¼ cup lemon juice
1 tablespoon drained capers

1. Place each salmon steak on 12-inch square of cheesecloth. Sprinkle with 1½ teaspoons salt, ⅛ teaspoon pepper, the dillweed, onion and parsley. Draw corners of cheesecloth to center and tie with string.

2. Pour ¾ cup water in cooker; heat to boiling. Place fish on rack in cooker.

3. Cover and set control at 10. Cook over high heat until pressure is reached. Reduce heat; cook 5 minutes (at 15 pounds pressure, cook 3½ minutes).

4. Cool cooker naturally.

5. Unwrap fish, let cool. Roll each pastry shell into circle on lightly-floured surface. Place one steak in center of each pastry circle. Fold pastry into packets by drawing pastry toward center of fish with points overlapping in center. Pat to seal.

6. Place packets on baking sheet, seam-sides-down. Cut slits in tops with knife; brush mixture of egg white and 1 tablespoon water over pastry.

7. Bake at 450°F until golden, 10 to 12 minutes.

8. Melt half the butter in cooker; stir in flour to form smooth paste. Remove from heat, stir in stock. Cook, stirring constantly, until thickened. Stir in ½ teaspoon salt, ⅛ teaspoon pepper, and the lemon juice. Stir in remaining butter, a tablespoon at a time.

9. Place fish on platter; spoon sauce over. Garnish with capers.

Makes 4 servings

Tips:

You can substitute wine or fish stock for part or all of the water specified in fish recipes.

Cooking times given in fish recipes can only be approximate, since even fish of the same weight will vary in size. You can check fish for doneness before end of cooking time by reducing pressure as indicated in recipe and piercing fish with a fork; it should flake easily. If fish is not done, bring cooker back up to pressure and cook a minute or two longer.

Haddock Stuffed with Oysters

Cook under pressure at 10 lbs. for 4 to 5 minutes (or at 15 lbs. for 3 to 4 minutes).

An Eastern specialty, particularly along the coast of Maine, this unusual fish dish has a provocative blend of flavors.

6 oysters
½ cup crushed oyster crackers
½ teaspoon salt
⅛ teaspoon pepper
1 tablespoon minced parsley
2 tablespoons butter or margarine, melted
2 haddock fillets, about 1 pound
1 tablespoon lemon juice
1 tablespoon butter or margarine, melted
¼ cup dry white wine
¼ cup water
Parsley

1. Drain and chop oysters; mix with cracker crumbs, salt, pepper, 1 tablespoon parsley, and 2 tablespoons of the butter.

2. Place 1 fish fillet on large piece of aluminum foil; sprinkle with lemon juice. Spoon oyster mixture over fish; place second fish fillet on top. Brush with remaining butter. Bring sides of foil up around fish, leaving top open.

3. Pour wine and water into cooker. Set fish packet on rack in cooker.

4. Cover and set control at 10. Cook over high heat until pressure is reached. Reduce heat; cook 4 to 5 minutes (at 15 pounds pressure, cook 3 to 4 minutes).

5. Reduce pressure at once by placing cooker under cold, running water.

6. Arrange fish carefully on platter. Garnish with parsley.

Makes 2 to 4 servings

Chinese~Steamed Smelts

Cook under pressure at 10 lbs. for 2 minutes (or at 15 lbs. for 1½ minutes).

Chinese fish specialties are always moist, fresh and light in taste. To fillet smelts, slit them lengthwise along the back and remove bone; open the small fish gently.

2 pounds smelts, filleted
1 teaspoon vegetable oil
1½ cups white distilled vinegar
1 cup soy sauce
2 tablespoons sugar
½ teaspoon sesame or vegetable oil
4 green onions, thinly sliced
1½ teaspoons minced fresh or canned gingerroot
Lemon wedges

1. Wash smelts; pat dry. Place fish in cooker greased with 1 teaspoon vegetable oil. Mix vinegar, soy sauce, sugar and sesame oil; pour over fish. Sprinkle with green onions and ginger.

2. Cover and set control at 10. Cook over high heat until pressure is reached. Reduce heat; cook 2 minutes (at 15 pounds pressure, cook 1½ minutes).

3. Reduce pressure at once by placing cooker under cold, running water.

4. Serve hot or cold. Garnish with lemon wedges.

Makes 4 to 6 servings

Fillets of Sole Marguery

Cook under pressure at 10 lbs. for 3 minutes (or at 15 lbs. for 2 minutes). Include an extra 15 minutes for baking fish casserole.

An accompaniment of shellfish and a sauce enriched with egg yolks are the hallmarks of this wonderful French dish.

4 sole fillets, about 4 ounces each
1 cup fish stock or clam juice
1 cup water
½ teaspoon salt
⅛ teaspoon white pepper
4 cooked shrimp
4 raw oysters
¼ cup dry white wine
4 tablespoons butter or margarine
2 egg yolks

1. Fold each fillet in half; place in greased casserole or oven-proof bowl; add fish stock. Cover casserole with aluminum foil; seal edges.

2. Add water to cooker. Place casserole on rack in cooker.

3. Cover and set control at 10. Cook over high heat until pressure is reached. Reduce heat; cook 3 minutes (at 15 pounds pressure, cook 2 minutes).

4. Reduce pressure at once by placing cooker under cold, running water.

5. Remove casserole and water from cooker. Strain fish stock into cooker. Sprinkle fish fillets with salt and pepper and top each fillet with a shrimp and an oyster.

6. Simmer stock in cooker until reduced to ¼ cup. Stir in 2 tablespoons wine and the butter. Cook over low heat until butter is melted.

7. Beat egg yolks until thick and lemon colored; stir in remaining wine. Add egg yolk mixture to cooker gradually. Cook, stirring constantly, until thickened.

8. Spoon sauce over fillets. Place casserole in oven and bake at 350° F until golden, about 15 minutes.

Makes 4 servings

Tip:
Always check the vent tube by holding the cover up to the light before using pressure cooker; light should be visible through the tube.

Shrimp~Stuffed Sole

Cook under pressure at 10 lbs. for 3 minutes (or at 15 lbs. for 2 minutes).

Sole stuffed with shrimp enhanced with just the right seasonings and cooked under pressure will yield a delicious lunch or dinner.

2 tablespoons lemon juice
¼ pound raw shrimp, shelled and deveined
4 sole fillets (about 4 ounces each)
½ teaspoon salt
⅛ teaspoon white pepper
¼ teaspoon dried dillweed
4 lemon slices
¼ cup dry white wine
1 cup hot water
    Parsley

1. Sprinkle lemon juice over shrimp; divide shrimp on fillets; sprinkle with salt, pepper and dillweed. Roll fillets; secure with toothpicks. Place fillets seam-sides-down on rack in cooker. Top fillets with lemon slices; pour wine and water over.

2. Cover and set control at 10. Cook over high heat until pressure is reached. Reduce heat; cook 3 minutes (at 15 pounds pressure, cook 2 minutes).

3. Reduce pressure at once by placing cooker under cold, running water.

4. Place fish on platter; garnish with parsley.

Makes 4 servings

Fillets of Sole Melinda

Cook under pressure at 10 lbs. for 3 minutes (or at 15 lbs. for 2 minutes).

An unusual combination of a bland white fish with sweet fruit gives this special dish a kind of South Seas feeling.

1½ cups pitted prunes
2 cups boiling water
1 can (13 ½ ounces) pineapple chunks, undrained
1 tablespoon minced parsley
1 bay leaf, crumbled
6 whole peppercorns
½ teaspoon salt
6 sole fillets
2 tablespoons butter or margarine
1 tablespoon all-purpose flour

1. Cover prunes with boiling water; let stand 30 minutes. Drain; reserve ½ of liquid. Drain pineapple chunks; combine syrup with enough prune liquid to make 1½ cups. Pour liquid into cooker. Stir in parsley, bay leaf, peppercorns and salt; heat to boiling. Remove cooker from heat.

2. Roll fillets; secure with toothpicks. Place fillets in cooker.

3. Cover and set control at 10. Cook over high heat until pressure is reached. Reduce heat; cook 3 minutes (at 15 pounds pressure, cook 2 minutes).

4. Reduce pressure at once by placing cooker under cold, running water.

5. Remove fish to platter; keep warm. Reserve 1 cup cooking liquid.

6. Melt butter in cooker; stir in flour to make smooth paste. Remove from heat. Stir in reserved cooking liquid gradually. Cook, stirring constantly, until thickened. Stir in prunes and pineapple chunks. Cook 3 minutes. Serve over fish.

Makes 6 servings

Trout Amandine

Cook under pressure at 10 lbs. for 4 minutes (or at 15 lbs. for 3 minutes).

A delicacy at any time — enjoy this superb combination year round with either freshly-caught or frozen trout.

2 fresh or frozen, thawed trout
½ cup yellow cornmeal
½ teaspoon salt
¼ teaspoon pepper
6 tablespoons butter or margarine
1 package (2½ ounces) blanched, sliced almonds
1 cup dry white wine
2 tablespoons lemon juice
Lemon wedges

1. Coat the trout with mixture of cornmeal, salt and pepper.

2. Heat 3 tablespoons of the butter in cooker; sauté almonds until golden; remove and reserve.

3. Add remaining butter to cooker; cook trout until golden on each side. Pour in wine; top with almonds.

4. Cover and set control at 10. Cook over high heat until pressure is reached. Reduce heat; cook 4 minutes (at 15 pounds pressure, cook 3 minutes).

5. Reduce pressure at once by placing cooker under cold, running water.

6. Arrange trout on platter; keep warm. (If a crisp coating is desired, place trout in baking pan and place under broiler about 2 minutes.)

7. Stir lemon juice into liquid in cooker; heat to boiling. Cook until sauce begins to thicken; serve over fish. Garnish with lemon wedges.

Makes 2 servings

Mackerel with Mustard Butter

Cook under pressure at 10 lbs. for 5 to 8 minutes (or at 15 lbs. for 4 to 6 minutes).

Bring out the finest flavor of this firm, rich fish by seasoning it with herbs and serving it in a sherry wine sauce.

2½ to 3 pound whole or half mackerel, dressed
1 teaspoon salt
¼ teaspoon pepper
⅛ teaspoon dried oregano leaves
2 tablespoons chopped parsley
1 tablespoon olive or vegetable oil
1 tablespoon Dijon-style mustard
2 tablespoons butter or margarine
1 cup dry sherry
2 tablespoons all-purpose flour
¼ cup water
6 sliced stuffed green olives

1. Rub surface of fish with mixture of salt, pepper, oregano, parsley, oil, mustard and butter. Place fish on rack in cooker; add sherry.

2. Cover and set control at 10. Cook over high heat until pressure is reached. Reduce heat; cook 5 to 8 minutes (at 15 pounds pressure, cook 4 to 6 minutes).

3. Reduce pressure at once by placing cooker under cold, running water.

4. Remove fish to a platter; keep warm. Measure 1 cup cooking liquid into cooker, heat to boiling. Mix flour and water; stir into cooker. Cook, stirring constantly, until sauce thickens.

5. Serve sauce over fish; garnish with olives.

Makes 6 servings

Bo'sun Stew

Cook under pressure at 10 lbs. for 6 minutes (or at 15 lbs. for 5 minutes).

A tangy fish dish that is easy to prepare and surprisingly flavored will prove even more delectable when served with a complementary dry white wine.

2 tablespoons butter or margarine
1½ cups coarsely-chopped onion
1 cup chopped celery
1½ cups catsup
1½ tablespoons steak sauce
⅛ teaspoon Worcestershire sauce
½ cup lime juice
½ teaspoon salt
⅛ teaspoon white pepper
1 pound frozen cod or sole fillets, slightly thawed
Lime wedges

1. Heat butter in cooker; sauté onion and celery until onion is tender. Stir in remaining ingredients except fish and lime wedges; cook 1 minute.
2. Cut fish into pieces, about 1½ x 4 inches. Gently place fish in sauce.
3. Cover and set control at 10. Cook over high heat until pressure is reached. Reduce heat; cook 6 minutes (at 15 pounds pressure, cook 5 minutes).
4. Reduce pressure at once by placing cooker under cold, running water.
5. Serve in shallow bowls; garnish with lime wedges.

Makes 4 servings

Tip:
You can substitute one type of firm-fleshed fish fillet for another in fish recipes.

Stuffed Striped Bass

Cook under pressure at 10 lbs. for 8 to 10 minutes (or at 15 lbs. for 6 to 8 minutes).

Fresh bass is delicious just about any way that you may wish to serve it, but for something special try it with this stuffing.

2½ pound striped bass, dressed
3 tablespoons butter or margarine
¼ cup minced onion
¾ cup finely-chopped mushrooms
1 stalk celery, cut into ½-inch pieces
1 large tomato, peeled, seeded, chopped
½ teaspoon chopped chives
1 tablespoon chopped parsley
½ cup French bread crumbs
½ teaspoon salt
⅛ teaspoon dried thyme leaves
⅛ teaspoon pepper
1 cup water
1 tablespoon lemon juice
⅓ cup dry white wine
1 tablespoon butter or margarine
Parsley
Lemon slices

1. Cut fish lengthwise along belly. Wash fish thoroughly.
2. Heat 3 tablespoons butter in cooker; sauté onion until tender. Stir in mushrooms and celery; cook 1 minute. Stir in tomato, chives, parsley, bread crumbs, salt, thyme and pepper; cool.
3. Stuff fish loosely with bread mixture; secure opening with skewers. Place fish on rack in cooker; pour in water. Drizzle lemon juice and wine over fish; dot with 1 tablespoon butter.
4. Cover and set control at 10. Cook over high heat until pressure is reached. Reduce heat; cook 8 to 10 minutes (at 15 pounds pressure, cook 6 to 8 minutes).
5. Reduce pressure at once by placing cooker under cold, running water.
6. Place fish on platter. Garnish with parsley and lemon slices.

Makes 4 servings

Halibut with Grapes

Cook under pressure at 10 lbs. for 5 to 6 minutes (or at 15 lbs. for 4 to 5 minutes).

Grapes in a creamy sauce add a special highlight to the natural sweetness of halibut. The sauce is easy to make with canned soup and sherry.

2 tablespoons butter or
   margarine
2 pounds halibut steaks
½ cup dry sherry
½ cup water
½ pound green seedless grapes
1 can (10½ ounces) cream of
   mushroom soup
1 tablespoon instant onion
   Minced parsley

1. Heat butter in cooker; cook fish 1 minute on each side. Remove fish carefully; place on rack in cooker. Pour in water.
2. Mix remaining ingredients, except parsley; pour over fish.
3. Cover and set control at 10. Cook over high heat until pressure is reached. Reduce heat; cook 5 to 6 minutes (at 15 pounds pressure, cook 4 to 5 minutes).
4. Reduce pressure at once by placing cooker under cold, running water.
5. Place fish on platter; spoon sauce over. Garnish with parsley.

Makes 4 to 6 servings

Tip:
Cooking times given in fish recipes can only be approximate, since even fish of the same weight will vary in size. You can check fish for doneness before end of cooking time by reducing pressure as indicated in recipe and piercing fish with a fork; it should flake easily. If fish is not done, bring cooker back up to pressure and cook a minute or two longer.

Halibut in Soy~Lemon Sauce

Cook under pressure at 15 lbs. for 0 minutes.

A light and elegant first course that takes almost no time to prepare. What a lovely way to start a meal!

1 pound fresh or frozen,
   thawed, halibut
1 cup dry white wine
4 cups shredded lettuce
1 large carrot, shredded
1 small cucumber, thinly sliced
½ cup lemon juice
½ cup soy sauce
⅓ cup chopped leek

1. Cut fish into thin slices; wrap in large square of cheesecloth. Place fish on rack in cooker; add wine.
2. Cover and set control at 15. Cook over high heat until pressure is reached. Reduce heat; cook 0 minutes. Cool cooker at once by placing cooker under cold, running water.
3. Carefully remove cheesecloth from fish. Refrigerate fish until chilled, about 1 hour.
4. Arrange lettuce on platter or individual plates; sprinkle carrot over. Arrange fish on lettuce; garnish with cucumber slices.
5. Mix lemon juice, soy sauce and leek; drizzle 2 tablespoons over fish. Pass remaining sauce.

Makes 4 to 6 servings

Halibut in Yogurt~Cheese Sauce

Cook under pressure at 10 lbs. for 13 minutes (or at 15 lbs. for 10 minutes). (See recipe how-to on page 74.)

A delicate yogurt-cheese sauce blankets these halibut steaks with a marvelous flavor. Paprika contributes rich color.

2 pounds halibut steaks, ½-inch thick
1 teaspoon salt
⅛ teaspoon white pepper
¼ teaspoon dried dillweed
1 cup yogurt
1 cup shredded Cheddar cheese
¼ teaspoon paprika
1 cup water
Parsley

1. Wash halibut steaks and pat dry with paper towels. Sprinkle fish with salt, pepper, and dillweed; place each steak on a large square of aluminum foil. Spread yogurt over fish; sprinkle with cheese and paprika.

2. Bring sides of foil up around fish, leaving top open. Pour water into cooker. Place fish packets on rack in cooker.

3. Cover and set control at 10. Cook over medium-high heat until pressure is reached. Reduce heat; cook 13 minutes (at 15 pounds pressure, cook about 10 minutes).

4. Reduce pressure at once by placing cooker under cold, running water.

5. Arrange fish on platter; spoon sauce over. Garnish with parsley.

Makes 4 servings

Scallops à la David Narsai

Cook under pressure at 10 lbs. for 3 minutes (or at 15 lbs. for 2 minutes). (See recipe how-to on page 73.)

This is a pressure cooker adaptation of a recipe created by famed Kensington, California restauranteur David Narsai.

3 ounces anise-flavored liqueur
⅔ cup dry white wine
½ cup water
1 onion, finely chopped
2 carrots, thinly sliced
2 stalks celery, chopped
1½ pounds scallops
½ teaspoon salt
⅛ teaspoon white pepper
1 tablespoon butter or margarine

1. Heat liqueur, wine and water to boiling in cooker. Stir in onion, carrots and celery. Stir in scallops, salt and pepper.

2. Cover and set control at 10. Cook over high heat until pressure is reached. Reduce heat; cook 3 minutes (at 15 pounds pressure, cook 2 minutes).

3. Reduce pressure at once by placing cooker under cold, running water.

4. Spoon scallops onto platter; keep warm. Add butter to liquid in cooker. Heat to boiling. Cook, stirring constantly, until sauce is reduced by half. Pour sauce over scallops.

Makes 4 servings

Fish Mushroom Rolls

Cook under pressure at 10 lbs. for 3 minutes (or at 15 lbs. for 2 minutes).

Combine fresh mushrooms and dill in a savory filling for rolled fish fillets. Serve these as a first course or an entrée.

1 tablespoon vegetable oil
8 fresh mushrooms, minced
4 large sandab or whitefish fillets
¼ teaspoon dried dillweed
1 can (10½ ounces) cream of mushroom soup
¾ cup water
1 tablespoon sherry
Parsley

1. Heat oil in cooker; sauté mushrooms 1 minute. Spoon mushrooms on each fillet. Sprinkle with dillweed.

2. Roll fillets; secure with toothpicks. Place fillets seam-sides-down on greased rack in cooker. Spoon half the mushroom soup over fish. Pour in water.

3. Cover and set control at 10. Cook over high heat until pressure is reached. Reduce heat; cook 3 minutes (at 15 pounds pressure, cook 2 minutes).

4. Reduce pressure at once by placing cooker under cold, running water.

5. Gently place fish on platter.

6. Heat remaining mushroom soup with sherry until hot; serve over fish. Garnish with parsley.

Makes 4 servings

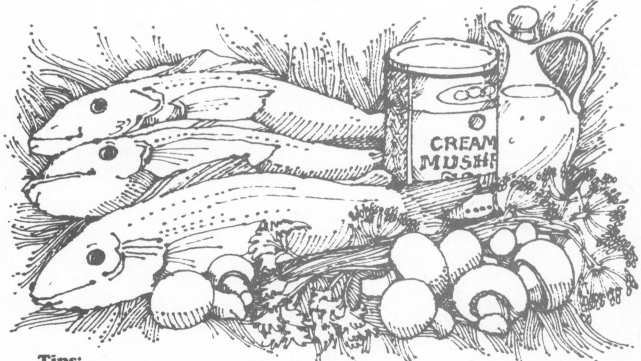

Tips:
You can substitute wine or fish stock for part or all of the water specified in fish recipes.

Cooking times given in fish recipes can only be approximate, since even fish of the same weight will vary in size. You can check fish for doneness before end of cooking time by reducing pressure as indicated in recipe and piercing fish with a fork; it should flake easily. If fish is not done, bring cooker back up to pressure and cook a minute or two longer.

Always reduce heat once pressure has been reached.

Recipe How-To's

To make the most of your pressure cooker, refer to these illustrated examples of the techniques you'll need for all kinds of recipes—from rich soups and tantalizing entrées to complete meals, delicate custards, breads, canned foods and pressure-fried specialties.

SOUPS: Carrot Potage (See complete recipe on page 24.)

Place carrots and salt in cooker. Pour in water. Cover and set control at 15. Cook over high heat until pressure is reached. Reduce heat; cook 1½ minutes.

Reserve 6 cooked carrot slices for garnish. Purée remaining carrots and liquid in food processor or blender.

Heat butter in cooker; stir in flour and cayenne to make a thick paste. Stir in milk gradually. Cook, stirring constantly, until mixture thickens.

Recipe How-To's

Carrot Potage (Continued)

Stir in carrot purée; then simmer gently for 20 minutes, stirring occasionally. Pour soup into bowls and garnish with carrot slices and parsley.

SOUPS: Portuguese Soup (See complete recipe on page 24.)

Place beef, onion, garlic, corn, parsley, salt, coriander, pepper, bay leaf, tomato sauce and water in cooker.

After beef, seasonings and other vegetables have cooked for 25 minutes, add potato and chard; then cook another 1½ minutes.

Before serving, stir wine into soup and heat uncovered. Top each serving of soup with a slice of toasted, buttered French bread.

Delicious, stew-like Portuguese Soup is crowned with a round of toasted French bread.

MEAT: Stuffed Cabbage (See complete recipe on page 36.)

Place cored head of cabbage in cooker. Pour boiling water over cabbage and let stand until cool. Then drain and separate leaves.

Spoon about 2 tablespoons of beef mixture filling onto each cabbage leaf. Fold in ends and roll up leaf.

Place cabbage rolls, seam-sides down, on rack in cooker. Pressure cooking the rolls in beef stock adds to their flavor.

Stuffed Cabbage (Continued)

Stir tomatoes, tomato sauce, sugar and salt into the cooking liquid to make a sauce for the cabbage rolls. Then simmer the rolls in the sauce without pressure. Spoon sauce over Stuffed Cabbage to serve.

MEAT: Quick Lamb Curry (See complete recipe on page 37.)

Heat vegetable oil in cooker; sauté sliced celery and chopped onion until tender.

Stir flour and curry powder into sautéed vegetables.

Stir beef stock, catsup and salt into the sautéed celery and onions. Then add cubed lamb, apples and raisins.

Serve Quick Lamb Curry with rice and condiments such as chopped apples, peanuts and sliced almonds.

MEAT: Polynesian Pork (See complete recipe on page 39.)

Cut a 2-pound piece of boneless pork tenderloin lengthwise into 2 strips.

Rub a marinade of sherry, salt, pineapple juice, soy sauce, cinnamon, cloves and sugar over all surfaces of the meat.

Let pork tenderloin stand for 10 minutes after cooking to make slicing easier; then cut into ¼-inch slices.

Recipe How-To's

Polynesian Pork (Continued)

Arrange pork tenderloin on a platter with pineapple and orange slices. Serve with mustard and soy sauce.

MEAT: Stuffed Pork Chops (See complete recipe on page 40.)

Have butcher cut pockets in 1-inch thick pork chops. Then stuff the chops with a mixture of rye bread crumbs, onion, caraway and other seasonings.

Close the pork chop pockets around the stuffing and secure with toothpicks.

Sprinkle stuffed chops with salt and pepper and dust with flour. Brown chops in cooker on both sides.

Stuffed Pork Chops (Continued)

Place browned chops on rack in cooker. Pour in 1 cup of water. The hearty Stuffed Pork Chops feature the wonderful spiciness of caraway.

CHICKEN: South Seas Chicken (See complete recipe on page 53.)

Heat vegetable oil in the pressure cooker and sauté ½-inch strips of skinned and boned chicken breasts.

Place chicken on rack in cooker and add ½ cup water. Then spoon orange and pineapple juice concentrates over chicken.

Remove chicken to serving platter. Then thicken 1 cup of the cooking liquid with arrowroot dissolved in water.

South Seas Chicken (Continued)

Stir drained pineapple tidbits, mandarin oranges and slivered almonds into thickened cooking liquid and cook 2 minutes over low heat. Then add sherry to sauce and serve over chicken.

CHICKEN: Chicken-Avocado Supreme (See complete recipe on page 52.)

Heat vegetable oil in cooker. Cook boned and skinned chicken breast halves in oil until brown on both sides.

Place chicken on rack in cooker. Pour in 1 cup of water.

Place each cooked chicken breast half on a square of foil. Bring up sides of foil to form a packet, leaving the top open.

Chicken-Avocado Supreme (Continued)

Place 2 slices of avocado on top of chicken in each packet. Arrange sliced olives and a tomato wedge on each. Before serving, arrange chicken on a heat-proof platter, sprinkle with cheese and place under broiler until cheese melts.

FISH: Scallops À La David Narsai (See complete recipe on page 63.)

Heat liqueur, wine and water in cooker; then stir in chopped onion, carrots, celery, scallops, salt and pepper.

Remove scallops to serving platter. Then add butter to cooking liquid and reduce sauce by heating it before pouring over scallops.

Recipe How-To's

FISH: Halibut In Yogurt-Cheese Sauce (See complete recipe on page 63.)

Sprinkle halibut steaks with salt, white pepper and dillweed.

Place each steak on a large square of foil and spread yogurt over fish.

Sprinkle shredded Cheddar cheese over yogurt-topped steaks.

Bring sides of foil up around each steak, leaving tops open. Pour water into cooker before placing packets on rack. Cheddar cheese and paprika give the cooked halibut steaks a golden color.

VEGETABLES: Mushroom Enchiladas (See complete recipe on page 96.)

Melt butter in cooker and sauté thickly-sliced fresh mushrooms until golden.

Stir chilies, onion, cream cheese, yogurt and flour into the mushrooms. Cook over low heat, stirring until the cheese melts and mixture is bubbly.

Heat enchilada sauce in a small saucepan. Using tongs, dip a tortilla into the sauce and place on a plate.

Spoon cheese mixture over sauce-coated tortilla and roll up. Place tortillas seam-sides down on a piece of foil fitted into the pressure cooker.

Sprinkle layer of 6 tortillas with shredded Cheddar cheese. Add a second layer, spoon enchilada sauce over, and sprinkle with more cheese.

Recipe How-To's

VEGETABLES: Broccoli With Cheese (See complete recipe on page 84.)

Arrange cooked broccoli in a greased 1-quart, oven-proof casserole and top with cheese sauce.

Blend melted butter and bread crumbs and sprinkle over sauce. Cover casserole with foil and seal edges before placing in cooker. Sprinkle broccoli with paprika before serving.

DINNERS: Meatball Dinner (See complete recipe on page 122.)

Brown meatball in vegetable oil in cooker and remove. Then set rack in cooker and place meatball on rack. Pour in water.

Trim artichoke stem and leaves. Place artichoke on rack in cooker and sprinkle with salt.

Place lemon slice on top of brown sugar and raisin-stuffed apple. Wrap apple in foil packet, leaving top open, before placing in cooker.

The Mushroom-Stuffed Meatball, Artichoke and Baked Apple cook together in the same amount of time.

STEAMED BREADS: Boston Brown Bread (See complete recipe on page 113.)

Spoon bread dough into greased 1-pound 4-ounce size cans, filling one-half full. (Make sure that cans have no sharp edges and be very careful when greasing them.)	Cover each can with a double thickness of aluminum foil; tie with string to hold in place.	Place cans on rack, leaving at least ¾ inch of space between cans and sides of cooker. Pour in water. Steam breads two at a time if your cooker will not hold the full recipe.

Recipe How-To's

Boston Brown Bread (Continued)

Cover cooker but do not set control. Cook over medium heat for 30 minutes, allowing steam to escape from vent. Then set control and finish cooking. The Boston Brown Bread is rich with molasses, raisins and chopped nuts.

DESSERTS: Apricot-Almond Custard (See complete recipe on page 103.)

Scald milk and cool slightly. The scalded milk will have a slight "skin" on it. Grease the custard cups.

Beat eggs, sugar, apricot brandy and salt lightly to blend. Gradually add hot milk, stirring constantly.

Pour mixture into 6-ounce glass or ceramic custard cups. Sprinkle sliced almonds over each cup.

Recipe How-To's

Apricot-Almond Custard (Continued)

Cover each custard cup tightly with aluminum foil. Place cups on rack in cooker.

Pour in water. (Cook custards 2 at a time if using a 4-quart or smaller cooker.)

Sliced almonds in custard float to the surface. Garnish with toasted almonds if you wish.

LOW PRESSURE FRYING: Fried Chicken (See complete recipe on page 138.)

Dip chicken into a mixture of beaten egg and beer.

Roll each piece in flour mixed with seasonings. Shake off excess flour.

Drain fried chicken on a cookie sheet lined with several layers of paper toweling or newspaper.

Low pressure frying produces crisp, moist fried chicken. (Never try to deep fry in a regular pressure cooker.)

CANNING: Fresh Vegetable Melange (See complete recipe on page 151.)

Sauté zucchini, onions, green pepper and garlic in vegetable oil in a large saucepan for 5 minutes. Stir in tomatoes and seasonings and boil 2 to 3 minutes.

Ladle vegetable mixture into standard canning jars free of nicks or cracks.

Ladle the boiling vegetable liquid over the vegetables in jars, leaving ½-inch headspace.

Wipe rims of jars; then adjust lids according to manufacturer's directions for the type of jar you're using.

Place rack in cooker and add the amount of water recommended by the manufacturer for your size cooker. Place jars on rack.

Pressure canning is the only safe way to can herb-scented Garden Fresh Vegetable Melange.

Vegetables

VEGETABLES ARE the pride of the pressure cooker. It is in this area that the cooker's speed and uniform steam achieve results that cannot be matched any other way. The tantalizing color of fresh asparagus, green beans and broccoli is majestically preserved; the succulence of pressure-cooked corn on the cob is absolutely superb. Potatoes cook in minutes; beets come to the table with all their rich nutrients retained.

The recipes in this chapter, however, cover a range of vegetarian foods in addition to fresh vegetables. For the pressure cooker performs brilliantly with frozen vegetables, dried beans and lentils and pastas as well. And many of these can be combined in delicious pressure-cooked casseroles that remove the stigma of lengthy preparation from vegetarian cookery.

Fresh Vegetables

The pressure cooker allows you to control the temperature required for any volume of food much more precisely than conventional cooking does. And this is the key to perfect, crisp-tender fresh vegetables. If vegetables are subject to too much heat, they become limp and unappetizing and both color and nutrients are lost. But there's no reason for this to happen with pressure cooking because the temperature remains constant at pressure and because even if the pot is filled to capacity with asparagus, for example, each stalk is nevertheless cooking at the same rate. So all you have to control is the timing under pressure.

The chart on the following page will provide you with the approximate times needed for most vegetables. We say "approximate" because the time required will vary according to the thickness and age of the vegetables. Medium-size potatoes vary in thickness, as do broccoli stalks and virtually every other vegetable. If you're not certain how long to cook a specific vegetable, begin by following the time given in the chart — you won't be far off. If necessary, you can always add more water to the cooker, bring it back up to pressure, and cook the food longer. Cook vegetables at 15 pounds pressure and always reduce pressure as soon as cooking is completed by holding the cooker under cold, running water or by placing it in a pan of cool water. When the time specified is "0" minutes, bring the cooker up to pressure and then begin reducing pressure immediately. Any vegetables that have the same cooking time can be steamed together; flavors will not mingle.

Our vegetable chart gives preparation directions and amounts of water needed for 2 1/2- to 4-quart cookers and for 6- to 8-quart cookers. You can always substitute wine, bouillon, stock or any kind of fruit or vegetable juice for the water.

Frozen Vegetables

With the exception of corn on the cob, which must be at least partially defrosted to keep the kernels from bursting during cooking, frozen vegetables should not be thawed before cooking. Cook them at 15 pounds pressure in 1/2 cup of liquid. Few need to be cooked longer than 0 minutes—just bring them up to pressure and then begin reducing pressure immediately.

Dried Beans And Lentils

With a pressure cooker, you never have to soak dried beans and lentils overnight before using them in either a conventional or a pressure cooker recipe. Instead, place one cup beans in cooker with two cups of water and one tablespoon of vegetable oil (and one teaspoon of salt, if desired). Cover the cooker and set the control at 15. Cook over high heat until pressure is reached. Then remove the cooker from the heat and reduce pressure naturally. The drained beans are ready for use in any recipe. We have included the procedure in our recipes for Seasoned Lima Beans and Sweet and Sour Kidney Beans; you may follow the same par-cooking procedure with any of your own recipes.

Vegetables

Pasta And Noodles

We have been very pleased with the texture of pressure-cooked pasta and noodles. This is the procedure we follow: For every four ounces of pasta, use one quart of water, one teaspoon of salt and one tablespoon of vegetable oil. Place pasta, water, salt and oil in the cooker and bring to a boil.(When cooking delicate noodles, add them after the water has begun to boil.) Cover the cooker and set control at 15. Cook over medium heat until pressure is reached. Reduce heat; cook 1 minute. Reduce pressure immediately by placing the cooker under cold, running water. Drain the pasta and proceed with whatever recipe you wish. Never fill the cooker more than half full when cooking pasta and noodles; check the vent pipe after cooking.

Rice

You can cook rice in the pressure cooker but you won't save much time. We prefer the lighter and fluffier texture of conventionally-steamed rice. We do cook rice in the pressure cooker in combination with other foods, for the sake of convenience. And we pressure cook the rice for Parslied Rice Ring with Creamed Mushrooms because in this recipe the slightly sticky texture of the rice helps the mold hold its shape.

Vegetable Casseroles

You'll find the recipes in this chapter fascinatingly diverse. There are both side-dish specialties like Broccoli Souffle, Minted Cucumbers and Glazed Carrots with Mint as well as such vegetarian entrées as Mushroom Enchiladas and Noodles and Cheese. We've combined vegetables, used various cooking liquids and created many kinds of sauces and toppings to go with the vegetables. Many of these combinations are pressure-steamed in casseroles. You may use any oven-proof bowl for these; we have had excellent results with a 1-quart souffle dish and recommend this container because it has straight sides that allow for even heat conduction to the center of the dish.

If you simply want pressure-steamed vegetables, with all their natural flavor intact and little more than a pat of butter to enhance them, follow the directions given in our Vegetable Cooking Chart. When you want more elaborate fare, turn to our harvest of recipes.

VEGETABLE COOKING CHART

Fresh Vegetables and Preparation	Amount of Water		Minutes at 15 Pounds Pressure
	4½ Quart or Smaller Cooker	6-8 Quart Cooker	
Artichoke: Wash, cut off 1″ of stem and trim leaves if desired	¾ cup	1 cup	12
Asparagus: Wash, snap off tough ends	½ cup	½ cup	0
Beans, green or wax: Wash, trim ends	¼ cup	½ cup	0
Beets: Cut off tops, leaving 1 inch stem and root, wash. Cool after cooking and remove skin. Reheat, if desired	1 cup	1 cup	10-16 (depending on size)
Broccoli, flowerets: Wash thoroughly	½ cup	½ cup	0
Broccoli, full stalks: Remove large leaves, trim stalks and cut thick stalks in half lengthwise without severing halves, wash	½ cup	½ cup	1
Brussels Sprouts: Wash, trim stalks, remove discolored outer leaves	¾ cup	¾ cup	3
Cabbage, shredded: Remove wilted outer leaves and wash before shredding	½ cup	½ cup	2 (3 minutes for red cabbage)
Cabbage, wedges: Remove wilted outer leaves, core, wash, cut into 3-inch wedges	½ cup	½ cup	7
Carrots, sliced: Trim and scrape before slicing	¼ cup	½ cup	1

VEGETABLE COOKING CHART

Fresh Vegetables and Preparation	Amount of Water		Minutes at 15 Pounds Pressure
	4½ Quart or Smaller Cooker	6-8 Quart Cooker	
Carrots, whole or large cut in half: trim and scrape	¼ cup	½ cup	2
Cauliflower, flowerets: Cut off stem and leaves before breaking into flowerets, wash	½ cup	½ cup	2
Cauliflower, whole: Cut off stem and leaves, remove center of core, wash, cook on rack	1 cup	1 cup	6
Celery: Separate stalks, trim and wash well, cut large stalks in half or cut into 1-inch pieces	¼ cup	½ cup	1 (half stalks) 0 (1-inch pieces)
Corn on the Cob: Remove husks and silk, wash, cook on rack	1 cup	1 cup	5
Eggplant: Wash, pare if desired, cut into ½-inch slices, cook on rack	½ cup	½ cup	0
Kohlrabi: Remove tops and peel, cut into ½-inch slices or 1-inch cubes	½ cup	½ cup	4
Onions, small to medium whole: Peel, wash	¾ cup	1 cup	5-10 (depending on size)
Peas: Shell and wash	½ cup	½ cup	0
Potatoes, medium to large, cut in half: Peel, wash and cut; cook on rack	¾ cup	1 cup	6-7 (depending on size)
Potatoes, medium to large whole: Peel, wash, and cook on rack	¾ cup	1 cup	10-12 (depending on size)
Rutabagas and Turnips: Peel and wash, cut into ½-inch slices or 1-inch cubes	½ cup	¾ cup	5
Spinach or other greens: Wash thoroughly	½ cup	½ cup	0
Squash, Acorn: Cut in half and remove seeds, cook on rack	½ cup	½ cup	5
Squash, Summer or Zucchini: Wash, cut in 1-inch slices, cook on rack	½ cup	½ cup	0
Sweet Potatoes or Yams: Wash, peel, cut in quarters or halves; cook on rack	1 cup	1 cup	5 (quarters) 7 (halves)

Frozen Vegetables (Do not thaw frozen vegetables except corn on the cob, which must be thawed.)	Amount of Water		Minutes at 15 Pounds Pressure
	4½ Quart or Smaller Cooker	6-8 Quart Cooker	
Asparagus Spears or Cuts	½	½	0
Broccoli Spears or Cuts	½	½	0
Brussels Sprouts	½	½	1
Carrots	½	½	0
Cauliflower	½	½	0
Corn on the Cob	½	½	2
Corn, Whole Kernel	½	½	0
Green Beans, Any Style	½	½	0
Lima Beans, Small	½	½	0
Lima Beans, Large	½	½	2
Peas	½	½	0
Spinach	½	½	0

Asparagus with Citrus Dressing

Cook under pressure at 15 lbs. for 0 to 1 minute.

When asparagus is in season, enjoy it every way you can. We especially like it topped with a tangy dressing and chilled.

1 pound fresh asparagus,
   washed
½ cup water
3 tablespoons lemon juice
½ cup vegetable oil
3 tablespoons vinegar
¼ teaspoon salt
⅛ teaspoon pepper
   Paprika

1. Break off tough asparagus ends; discard. Place asparagus in cooker; pour in water.

2. Cover and set control at 15. Cook over high heat until pressure is reached. Reduce heat; cook 0 to 1 minute, depending upon size of stalks.

3. Reduce pressure at once by placing cooker under cold, running water.

4. Place asparagus in serving bowl. Mix lemon juice, oil, vinegar, salt, pepper and dash of paprika. Drizzle over asparagus. Let cool; refrigerate until serving time.

Makes 4 servings

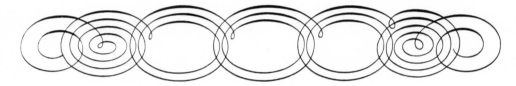

Broccoli with Cheese

Cook under pressure at 15 lbs. for 2 minutes. (See recipe how-to on page 76.)

Parboil broccoli; then pressure cook it in a casserole with cheese and seasonings for a quick lunch or a good accompaniment with pork or beef.

1 pound fresh broccoli, washed
½ cup water
½ teaspoon salt
1 egg, slightly beaten
½ cup cottage cheese
2 tablespoons instant minced
   onion
2 tablespoons shredded Swiss
   cheese
2 drops hot sauce
½ teaspoon salt
⅛ teaspoon white pepper
1 tablespoon butter or
   margarine, melted
3 tablespoons bread crumbs
1½ cups water
   Paprika

1. Cut off tough stems of broccoli; discard. Cut stalks in half lengthwise. Place broccoli, ½ cup water and ½ teaspoon salt in cooker. Heat to boiling; boil 3 minutes. Drain.

2. Arrange broccoli in greased 1-quart, oven-proof casserole.

3. Combine egg, cottage cheese, onion, Swiss cheese, hot sauce, ½ teaspoon salt and the pepper; pour over broccoli. Blend butter and bread crumbs. Sprinkle over broccoli. Cover casserole with aluminum foil and seal edges; place on rack in cooker. Pour in 1½ cups water.

4. Cover and set control at 15. Cook over high heat until pressure is reached. Reduce heat; cook 2 minutes.

5. Reduce pressure at once by placing cooker under cold, running water.

6. Remove foil and sprinkle broccoli with paprika.

Makes 4 servings

Broccoli Soufflé

Cook under pressure at 15 lbs. for 8 minutes.

Substitute spinach if you wish in this fluffy and elegant side dish or luncheon entrée. You could also use grated Swiss or Cheddar cheese instead of Parmesan.

1 teaspoon butter or margarine
1 teaspoon all-purpose flour
½ cup warm milk
⅛ teaspoon salt
⅛ teaspoon pepper
⅛ teaspoon ground nutmeg
2 large eggs, separated
1 package (10½ ounces) frozen chopped broccoli, thawed, squeezed dry
2 tablespoons grated Parmesan cheese
1½ cups water

1. Melt butter in small saucepan; stir in flour to make a smooth paste.

2. Stir milk gradually into flour mixture. Cook, stirring constantly, over medium heat until sauce is smooth and begins to thicken. Stir in salt, pepper and nutmeg; remove from heat.

3. Cool sauce slightly. Beat in yolks; stir in broccoli.

4. Beat egg whites until stiff, but not dry. Gently fold into broccoli mixture. Pour mixture into greased 1-quart mold or oven-proof casserole; sprinkle with cheese. Cover mold with aluminum foil; tie in place with string. Place rack in cooker; pour in water. Place mold on rack.

5. Cover and set control at 15. Cook over high heat until pressure is reached. Reduce heat; cook 8 minutes.

6. Reduce pressure at once by placing cooker under cold, running water.

Makes 2 to 3 servings

Tip:

Always check the vent tube by holding the cover up to the light before using pressure cooker; light should be visible through the tube.

Fruited Sweet Potatoes

Cook under pressure at 15 lbs. for 8 minutes.

An appropriate choice for any festive occasion, this treat is easy enough to prepare for everyday meals too. It's especially good with ham or pork.

4 large sweet potatoes, washed
1 cup hot water
2 tablespoons butter or margarine
½ cup orange juice
2 tblespoons lemon juice
⅛ teaspoon orange peel, grated
½ teaspoon salt
½ teaspoon ground cinnamon
⅓ cup golden raisins
⅓ cup crushed pineapple, drained
1 tablespoon brown sugar

1. Place potatoes on rack in cooker. Add water.

2. Cover and set control at 15. Cook over high heat until pressure is reached. Reduce heat; cook 8 minutes.

3. Reduce pressure at once by placing cooker under cold, running water.

4. Peel potatoes; mash until fluffy. Add butter, orange juice and lemon juice. Stir in orange peel, salt, cinnamon, raisins, pineapple and brown sugar.

5. Heat in cooker over low heat until hot, about 5 minutes. Stir occasionally to keep fluffy.

Makes 4 servings

Broccoli with Sherry~Walnut Sauce

Cook under pressure at 15 lbs. for 1 minute. Include an extra 15 minutes for baking broccoli.

A relative newcomer to the United States, broccoli was popular more than 2000 years ago in Greece and Italy. It's always delicious served simply with butter, but a sauce and a sprinkling of cheese make it superb.

1 pound fresh broccoli, washed
½ cup water
½ teaspoon salt
2 tablespoons butter or margarine
2 tablespoons all-purpose flour
1 cup beef stock or canned beef broth
½ cup cream or milk
2 tablespoons sherry
1 tablespoon lemon juice
½ teaspoon salt
⅛ teaspoon pepper
2 tablespoons shredded Cheddar cheese
2 tablespoons toasted, chopped walnuts

1. Cut off tough stems of broccoli; discard. Cut stalks in half lengthwise. Place broccoli, water and ½ teaspoon salt in cooker.

2. Cover and set control at 15. Cook over high heat until pressure is reached. Reduce heat; cook 1 minute.

3. Reduce pressure at once by placing cooker under cold, running water.

4. Place broccoli in greased 1-quart, oven-proof casserole.

5. Heat butter in cooker. Stir in flour to make smooth paste. Remove from heat; stir in stock and cream gradually. Return to heat and cook, stirring constantly, until mixture thickens. Stir in remaining ingredients, except cheese and nuts.

6. Pour sauce over broccoli. Sprinkle with cheese and nuts. Bake at 350°F until thoroughly hot and cheese is melted, about 15 minutes.

Makes 4 servings

Tip:

Cooking times given for vegetables can only be approximate, since size and age will affect timing. Times given will usually produce slightly crisp green vegetables; you may wish to add one or two minutes to cooking times.

Potato~Broccoli Casserole

Cook under pressure at 15 lbs. for 2 minutes. Include an extra 10 minutes for baking casserole.

Glistening carrots crown this attractive, inexpensive casserole of three vegetables. Cheddar cheese and dill bridge the flavors of potatoes and broccoli.

1 package (10¾ ounces) frozen, chopped broccoli
1 small carrot, sliced into ½ inch pieces
3 medium potatoes, pared, sliced

1. Place broccoli on square of aluminum foil; bring up sides to form packet, leaving top open. Place carrots on square of foil; bring up sides to form packet; leaving top open. Place potatoes on rack in cooker. Pour water into cooker. Place packets of broccoli and carrots in cooker.

Potato-Broccoli Casserole (Continued)

½ cup water
2 tablespoons butter or margarine
¼ to ½ cup warm milk
½ cup shredded sharp Cheddar cheese
1 teaspoon salt
¼ teaspoon white pepper
¼ teaspoon dried dillweed
2 tablespoons butter or margarine, melted
Brown sugar

2. Cover and set control at 15. Cook over high heat until pressure is reached. Reduce heat; cook 2 minutes.

3. Reduce pressure at once by placing cooker under cold, running water.

4. Mash potatoes with 2 tablespoons butter; add milk for desired consistency. Stir in cheese, salt, pepper and dillweed. Drain broccoli; stir into potatoes. Spoon potato mixture into greased casserole.

5. Roll carrots in melted butter; sprinkle with brown sugar. Arrange on potatoes.

6. Bake casserole in 350°F oven about 10 minutes to blend flavors and heat through.

Makes 4 servings

Tips:

Vegetables that require the same amount of cooking time may be cooked together; flavors will not mingle.

You can substitute bouillon, broth or wine for part or all of the water specified in vegetable recipes.   Always reduce heat once pressure has been reached.

Brussels Sprouts in Cheese Sauce

Cook under pressure at 15 lbs. for 2 to 3 minutes.

Rich in vitamins C and A, this diminutive member of the cabbage family is particularly pleasing dressed with a sharp cream cheese sauce. Choose small, compact Brussels sprouts for best results and do not wash and trim until ready to prepare.

1 pound Brussels sprouts
2 tablespoons sugar
½ teaspoon salt
⅛ teaspoon ground nutmeg, if desired
¾ cup boiling water

Cheese Sauce

1 package (8 ounces) cream cheese, softened
3 tablespoons sour cream
2 tablespoons cream or milk
1 teaspoon lemon juice
¼ teaspoon Worcestershire sauce
⅛ teaspoon salt
¼ cup chopped walnuts

1. Wash Brussels sprouts; trim stems and remove any discolored outer leaves. Mix sugar, ½ teaspoon salt and the nutmeg in cooker. Cook over medium heat until sugar begins to melt and turns brown. Immediately add sprouts and water.

2. Cover and set control at 15. Cook over high heat until pressure is reached. Reduce heat; cook 2 to 3 minutes, depending on size of Brussels sprouts.

3. Reduce pressure at once by placing cooker under cold, running water.

4. Drain sprouts; place in serving bowl and keep warm.

5. Mix cream cheese, sour cream and cream in cooker. Cook, stirring constantly, over low heat until heated. Stir in lemon juice, Worcestershire sauce and ⅛ teaspoon salt. Cook until warm, about 3 minutes.

6. Spoon sauce over sprouts; sprinkle nuts over top.

Makes 3 servings

Cauliflower with Mustard

Cook under pressure at 15 lbs. for 2 to 3 minutes.

If you like cauliflower with a slight crunch, cook the flowerets only two minutes. Mustard and paprika add a spicy accent and a dash of colorful contrast.

1 head cauliflower, stems and leaves removed, washed
½ cup water
½ teaspoon salt
¼ teaspoon dried oregano leaves
1 teaspoon prepared mustard
⅛ teaspoon paprika
3 tablespoons butter or margarine

1. Cut cauliflower into flowerets; place in cooker with water and salt.

2. Cover and set control at 15. Cook over high heat until pressure is reached. Reduce heat; cook 2 to 3 minutes.

3. Reduce pressure at once by placing cooker under cold, running water.

4. Drain cauliflower. Mix oregano, mustard, paprika and butter into smooth paste; spread over cauliflower.

Makes 4 servings

Far Eastern Cabbage

Cook under pressure at 15 lbs. for 1 minute, and then 2 minutes more.

Cabbage is such an adaptable vegetable and grows in so many parts of the world that it is universally popular. When you want a change of flavor, try it seasoned with curry and cayenne.

1 head cabbage
2 whole cloves
1 clove garlic
1 bay leaf
1 cup hot beef stock
2 tablespoons butter or margarine
3 tablespoons all-purpose flour
1½ teaspoons curry powder
½ teaspoon salt
⅛ teaspoon cayenne pepper
1 cup milk
⅓ cup shredded Cheddar cheese
Paprika
1 cup water

1. Shred cabbage and rinse. Tie cloves, garlic and bay leaf in cheesecloth; place in cooker with cabbage; add beef stock.

2. Cover and set control at 15. Cook over medium heat until pressure is reached. Reduce heat; cook 1 minute.

3. Reduce pressure at once by placing cooker under cold, running water.

4. Drain cabbage; discard spices. Heat butter in small saucepan. Stir in flour to form a smooth paste. Stir in curry, salt and cayenne. Remove from heat; stir in milk gradually. Cook, stirring constantly, until mixture thickens and begins to bubble.

5. Place half the cabbage in a greased metal mold or oven-proof casserole. Spoon half the sauce over cabbage; repeat layer. Sprinkle with cheese and paprika. Pour water into cooker. Set mold on rack in cooker.

6. Cover and set control at 15. Cook over high heat until pressure is reached. Reduce heat; cook 2 minutes.

7. Reduce pressure at once by placing cooker under cold, running water.

Makes 4 servings

Minted Cucumbers

Cook under pressure at 15 lbs. for 0 minutes.

This is a terrific way to serve cucumbers when the harvest is abundant and you want a change-of-pace dish. The cucumbers stay slightly crisp and the touch of mint is quite refreshing.

**2 medium cucumbers, pared
½ cup water
1 teaspoon salt
2 tablespoons butter or
    margarine
1½ teaspoons finely-chopped
    mint leaves
⅛ teaspoon pepper
¼ cup cider vinegar**

1. Cut cucumbers in half lengthwise; scoop out seeds. Cut cucumbers into 2-inch pieces. Place cucumbers, water and salt in cooker.

2. Cover and set control at 15. Cook over high heat until pressure is reached. Cook 0 minutes. Remove cooker from heat.

3. Reduce pressure at once by placing cooker under cold, running water.

4. Drain cucumbers and set aside. Heat butter in cooker. Stir in mint and pepper; sauté 1 minute. Stir in cucumbers and vinegar; cook until liquid boils.

Makes 4 servings

Tip:
Always check the vent tube by holding the cover up to the light before using pressure cooker; light should be visible through the tube.

Herbed Celery and Carrots

Cook under pressure at 15 lbs. for 1 minute.

A sauce made with dill and mozzarella cheese turns fresh celery and carrots into an exciting combination.

**4 small young carrots, washed,
    scraped
4 stalks celery, washed
½ cup water
1 teaspoon salt
1 tablespoon butter or
    margarine
1 tablespoon all-purpose flour
⅔ cup milk
⅛ teaspoon salt
⅛ teaspoon dried dillweed
2 tablespoons shredded
    mozzarella cheese
Paprika**

1. Cut carrots and celery into ¾-inch pieces. Place in cooker with water and 1 teaspoon salt.

2. Cover and set control at 15. Cook over high heat until pressure is reached. Reduce heat; cook 1 minute.

3. Reduce pressure at once by placing cooker under cold, running water.

4. Drain vegetables and reserve. Heat butter in cooker; stir in flour to make smooth paste. Remove from heat. Stir in milk gradually. Add ⅛ teaspoon salt and the dillweed.

5. Cook, stirring constantly, until sauce thickens. Add the mozzarella cheese; cook, stirring constantly, until cheese melts. Stir in vegetables; cook 1 minute. Serve in bowl; sprinkle with paprika.

Makes 4 servings

Glazed Carrots with Mint

Cook under pressure at 15 lbs. for 2 to 3 minutes.

A year round favorite, carrots cook beautifully in the pressure cooker. Small spring carrots are particularly suitable for glazing. Try brown sugar or maple sugar and honey instead of white sugar for the glaze.

12 small young carrots, tops removed, washed and scraped
⅛ teaspoon salt
½ cup hot water
2 tablespoons butter or margarine
1½ tablespoons brown sugar
1 tablespoon honey
1 tablespoon finely-chopped mint

1. Place carrots, salt and water in cooker.
2. Cover and set control at 15. Cook over high heat until pressure is reached. Reduce heat; cook 2 to 3 minutes, depending on size of carrots.
3. Reduce pressure at once by placing cooker under cold, running water.
4. Drain carrots; cut in half lengthwise. Heat butter in cooker; add sugar, honey and carrots; stir until carrots are coated with glaze. Sprinkle with mint.

Makes 3 to 4 servings

Carrot~Parsnip Pudding

Cook under pressure at 15 lbs. for 4 to 5 minutes.

Blend the flavors of carrots and parsnips with wine and herbs; then add whipped cream or yogurt for an elegant side dish purée.

4 medium parsnips or turnips, washed, pared, cut into fourths
4 long carrots, washed, scraped, cut into fourths
½ cup dry white wine
2 tablespoons lemon juice
½ teaspoon salt
¼ cup minced parsley
1 teaspoon dried thyme leaves
½ teaspoon salt
⅛ teaspoon pepper
½ cup whipping cream, whipped, or ½ cup yogurt
Parsley

1. Place vegetables on rack in cooker. Pour in wine, lemon juice and ½ teaspoon salt. Heat to boiling.
2. Cover and set control at 15. Cook over high heat until pressure is reached. Reduce heat; cook 4 to 5 minutes.
3. Reduce pressure immediately by placing cooker under cold, running water.
4. Purée vegetables with cooking liquid in blender or food processor; place in cooker. Stir in parsley, thyme, ½ teaspoon salt and the pepper. Fold in whipped cream.
5. Heat over low heat until hot, about 4 minutes.
6. Garnish with parsley.

Makes 4 servings

Marinated Carrots

Cook under pressure at 15 lbs. for 1 minute.

These spicy carrots are marvelous served as an hors d'oeuvre or with cold meats. Cooking time given will leave carrots crisp; cook longer, if you wish.

¼ cup vegetable oil
2 cloves garlic, minced

1. Heat oil in cooker; sauté garlic and onion until tender. Stir in remaining ingredients.

Marinated Carrots (Continued)

1 small onion, finely chopped
4 large carrots, trimmed, scraped, thinly sliced
1½ tablespoons whole pickling spice
1½ teaspoons salt
1 teaspoon prepared mustard
2 tablespoons catsup
⅛ teaspoon pepper
⅓ cup wine vinegar
2 tablespoons hot water

2. Cover and set control at 15. Cook over medium-high heat until pressure is reached. Reduce heat; cook 1 minute.

3. Reduce pressure at once by placing cooker under cold, running water.

4. Partially drain carrots; refrigerate until chilled.

5. Spear with toothpicks to serve as an hors d'oeuvre, or drain completely and serve as a relish.

Makes about 2 cups

Green Beans with Almonds

Cook under pressure at 15 lbs. for 0 minutes.

Sharpen the flavor of fresh green beans with a subtle touch of marjoram, the tartness of lemon juice and the crunch of almonds.

1½ tablespoons butter or margarine
½ cup slivered, blanched almonds
1½ pounds fresh green beans, washed, ends trimmed
½ teaspoon salt
⅛ teaspoon dried marjoram leaves
½ cup water
1 teaspoon lemon juice

1. Heat butter in cooker; sauté almonds until light brown. Remove almonds and reserve. Place beans, salt, marjoram and water in cooker.

2. Cover and set control at 15. Cook over high heat until pressure is reached. Cook 0 minutes. Remove cooker from heat.

3. Reduce pressure at once by placing cooker under cold, running water.

4. Drain beans. Add almonds and lemon juice; toss to blend. *Makes 4 servings*

Green Beans with Water Chestnuts

Cook under pressure at 15 lbs. for 0 minutes.

Add peanuts, if you wish, for unusual texture and flavor. The combination of beans, leeks and water chestnuts is also deliciously crunchy by itself.

1 tablespoon butter or margarine
2 leek stalks, split, washed and cut into ½-inch pieces
½ cup sliced, fresh mushrooms
1 tablespoon minced onion
⅓ cup coarsely-chopped peanuts, if desired
1½ pounds green beans, washed, ends trimmed
½ teaspoon salt
½ cup water
¼ cup thinly-sliced water chestnuts

1. Heat butter in cooker. Sauté leeks, mushrooms and onion until limp. Add peanuts, beans, salt and water.

2. Cover and set control at 15. Cook over high heat until pressure is reached. Cook 0 minutes. Remove cooker from heat.

3. Reduce pressure at once by placing cooker under cold, running water.

4. Stir in water chestnuts. Heat over medium heat until hot.

Makes 4 servings

Italian~Style Green Beans

Cook under pressure at 15 lbs. for 0 minutes.

A fresh tomato sauce, seasoned with onion, garlic and basil, turns crisp green beans into a wonderfully fragrant side dish.

1 pound fresh green beans,
    washed, ends trimmed
½ cup water
1½ tablespoons vegetable oil
1 small onion, minced
1 clove garlic, minced
2 ripe tomatoes, peeled,
    quartered
2 tablespoons tomato paste
½ teaspoon salt
⅛ teaspoon pepper
¼ teaspoon dried basil leaves
½ teaspoon sugar

1. Place green beans and water in cooker.
2. Cover and set control at 15. Cook over high heat until pressure is reached. Cook 0 minutes. Remove cooker from heat.
3. Reduce pressure at once by placing cooker under cold, running water.
4. Drain and reserve beans. Heat oil in cooker; sauté onion and garlic until tender.
5. Add tomatoes, tomato paste, salt, pepper, basil, and sugar. Cook, stirring occasionally, until tomatoes and liquid are reduced to a thick consistency. Stir in beans; cook 2 minutes.

Makes 4 servings

Tip:
Save time by parcooking dried beans and lentils in the pressure cooker instead of soaking them; see directions on page 81.

Seasoned Lima Beans

Cook under pressure at 15 lbs. for 0 minutes, then 10 minutes, and then 1 minute more.

Celery, green pepper, herbs and spices make these lima beans special. Add corn kernels near the end of cooking time, so that they don't overcook.

1 cup dried lima beans
2 cups water
1 tablespoon vegetable oil
1 teaspoon salt
1 tablespoon vegetable oil
2 tablespoons chopped celery
2 tablespoons chopped green
    pepper
2 tablespoons instant minced
    onion
1 clove garlic, peeled and
    minced
1 teaspoon salt
⅛ teaspoon ground mace
⅛ teaspoon dried basil leaves
1 teaspoon Worcestershire
    sauce
1 cup tomato juice
1 tablespoon vegetable oil
1 package (9 ounces) frozen
    whole kernel corn

1. Place the beans, water, 1 tablespoon oil and 1 teaspoon salt in cooker.
2. Cover and set control at 15. Cook over high heat until pressure is reached; cook 0 minutes. Reduce pressure naturally. Drain beans. Rinse out cooker and wipe dry.
3. Heat 1 tablespoon oil in cooker. Sauté celery, green pepper, onion and garlic until tender. Add lima beans and remaining ingredients except corn.
4. Cover and set control at 15. Cook over medium heat until pressure is reached. Reduce heat; cook 10 minutes.
5. Reduce pressure at once by placing cooker under cold, running water. Stir in corn.
6. Cover and set control at 15. Cook over high heat until pressure is reached. Reduce heat; cook 1 minute.
7. Reduce pressure at once by placing cooker under cold, running water.

Makes 3 to 4 servings

Eastern Succotash

Cook under pressure at 15 lbs. for 0 to 2 minutes.

Originally succotash was made with kidney beans and corn cooked in bear grease. We think our modern version improves on the Narragansett Indian dish with the substitution of lima beans and the addition of chopped tomato.

2 slices salt pork
1 pound shelled fresh lima beans, washed, or 1 package (10 ounces) frozen lima beans
4 ears corn, kernels cut from cob, or 1 package (10 ounces) frozen whole kernel corn
1 tablespoon butter or margarine
1 teaspoon salt
⅛ teaspoon pepper
½ cup water
1 tomato, peeled, chopped
Ground nutmeg, if desired

1. Cook salt pork in cooker until soft, about 2 minutes. Drain fat. Add remaining ingredients, except nutmeg.

2. Cover and set control at 15. Cook over high heat until pressure is reached. Reduce heat; cook 0 to 2 minutes, depending upon size of lima beans.

3. Reduce pressure at once by placing cooker under cold, running water.

4. Remove salt pork or cut into small cubes and stir into succotash. Sprinkle lightly with nutmeg; toss to blend.

Makes 3 to 4 servings

Sweet and Sour Kidney Beans

Cook under pressure at 15 lbs. for 0 minutes, and then 25 minutes more.

Save time by parcooking beans in pressure cooker instead of soaking them overnight. Then prepare nutritious kidney beans with a great blend of sweet and spicy seasonings.

1 cup dried kidney beans
2 cups water
1 tablespoon vegetable oil
2 cups water
1 tablespoon vegetable oil
1 tablespoon instant minced onion
½ cup packed brown sugar
1 tablespoon prepared mustard
¼ cup dry sherry
2 tablespoons cider vinegar
1 teaspoon salt
⅛ teaspoon black pepper
½ teaspoon instant dry coffee

1. Place beans, 2 cups water and 1 tablespoon oil in cooker.

2. Cover and set control at 15. Cook over high heat until pressure is reached. Cook 0 minutes. Reduce pressure naturally. Drain beans. Rinse out cooker and wipe dry.

3. Place beans, 2 cups water, 1 tablespoon oil and remaining ingredients in cooker.

4. Cover and set control at 15. Cook over medium-high heat until pressure is reached. Reduce heat; cook 25 minutes.

5. Cool cooker naturally 5 minutes; place cooker under cold, running water to complete pressure reduction.

Makes 4 servings

Tip:
Vegetables that require the same amount of cooking time may be cooked together; flavors will not mingle. Never fill cooker more than two-thirds full.

Italian~Style Stuffed Peppers

Cook under pressure at 15 lbs. for 5 to 6 minutes.

You'll love the combination of sardines, capers and olives that gives the stuffing for these peppers such true Italian flavor.

4 green bell peppers
1 tablespoon olive or vegetable oil
¼ cup chopped onion
1 cup sliced fresh mushrooms
1½ cups dry bread crumbs
4 sardines or anchovies, minced
1 tablespoon drained capers
2 tablespoons sliced black, pitted olives
⅛ teaspoon dried oregano leaves
3 tablespoons tomato paste
1 cup water

1. Slice tops off stem ends of the peppers; remove seeds. Heat olive oil in cooker; sauté onion and mushrooms until onion is tender. Stir in remaining ingredients except water.

2. Stuff peppers with mushroom mixture. Pour water into cooker. Place peppers on rack in cooker.

3. Cover and set control at 15. Cook over high heat until pressure is reached. Reduce heat; cook 5 to 6 minutes, depending on size of peppers.

4. Reduce pressure at once by placing cooker under cold, running water.

Makes 4 servings

Eggplant~Sprouts Casserole

Cook under pressure at 15 lbs. for 5 minutes.

This is a treasury of fresh vegetables that combines eggplant, bean sprouts and tomatoes with Italian-style seasonings. Try it with broiled Italian sausage and crusty bread for a quick dinner.

Boiling water (enough to cover)
1 medium eggplant, pared, finely chopped
3 tablespoons butter or margarine
1 cup chopped soybean or mung bean sprouts
1 cup chopped celery
1 cup coarsely-chopped onion
1 cup peeled, chopped tomato
1 egg, slightly beaten
½ teaspoon dried oregano leaves
1 teaspoon salt
¼ teaspoon white pepper
¾ cup seasoned dry bread crumbs
½ cup grated Parmesan cheese
1 cup warm water
1 teaspoon paprika

1. Pour boiling water over chopped eggplant in 1-quart oven-proof bowl; let stand 5 to 10 minutes; drain. Lightly grease bowl.

2. Heat butter in cooker; sauté sprouts, celery, onion, tomato and eggplant until onion is tender. Remove from heat. Stir in egg, oregano, salt, pepper and bread crumbs.

3. Press mixture into the oven-proof bowl; sprinkle half the Parmesan cheese over top. Cover the bowl loosely with aluminum foil and pinch edges tightly to rim. Pour water into cooker. Place bowl on rack in cooker.

4. Cover and set control at 15. Cook over high heat until pressure is reached. Reduce heat; cook 5 minutes.

5. Reduce pressure at once by placing cooker under cold, running water.

6. Sprinkle with remaining cheese and paprika; place under broiler until cheese browns, about 1 minute.

Makes 4 servings

Parslied Rice Ring with Creamed Mushrooms

Cook under pressure at 15 lbs. for 1 minute.

This is a festive-looking rice mold for special dinners. You can cook the parslied rice without shaping it in a mold for everyday enjoyment; serve it with or without the mushroom sauce.

1 cup uncooked parboiled rice
2½ cups water
1 teaspoon salt
2 tablespoons lemon juice
1 tablespoon butter or
    margarine
2 tablespoons chopped parsley
1 teaspoon grated lemon peel
1 can (10½ ounces) cream of
    mushroom soup
2 tablespoons heavy cream or
    milk
2 tablespoons dry sherry
1 can (4 ounces) sliced
    mushrooms, drained
    Parmesan cheese, grated

1. Mix rice, water, salt, lemon juice and butter in cooker.

2. Cover and set control at 15. Cook over medium heat until pressure is reached. Reduce heat; cook 1 minute.

3. Cool cooker naturally 5 minutes; reduce pressure completely by placing cooker under cold, running water. Remove cover. Stir in parsley and lemon peel. Let stand until water is absorbed, about 5 minutes.

4. Press rice into a small, greased ring mold.

5. Heat mushroom soup, cream, sherry, and mushrooms in cooker to boiling. Unmold rice ring onto serving plate; spoon mushroom mixture into center of ring. Sprinkle with Parmesan cheese.

Makes 4 servings

Mushrooms Stuffed with Spinach

Cook under pressure at 15 lbs. for 0 minutes.

You can serve these stuffed mushrooms as either an appetizer or a side dish. They are an especially savory version of an ever popular dish.

12 large fresh mushrooms
1 tablespoon butter or
    margarine
1 tablespoon grated onion
2 tablespoons sweet vermouth
1 tablespoon minced parsley
1 teaspoon anchovy paste
½ cup frozen chopped spinach,
    thawed, water squeezed out
1 tablespoon cream or milk
⅛ teaspoon pepper
    Dash nutmeg
    Parmesan cheese, grated
½ cup water

1. Remove stems from mushrooms; scoop out caps. Mince inside of caps and stems; reserve caps. Melt butter in cooker; sauté minced mushrooms and onion about 2 minutes; remove cooker from heat.

2. Stir vermouth, parsley and anchovy paste into mushroom mixture. When smooth, stir in spinach, cream, pepper and nutmeg.

3. Fill each mushroom cap with spinach mixture. Sprinkle with Parmesan cheese. Pour water into cooker. Set stuffed mushrooms on rack in cooker.

4. Cover and set control at 15. Cook over high heat until pressure is reached. Cook 0 minutes. Remove cooker from heat.

5. Reduce pressure at once by placing cooker under cold, running water.

Makes 3 to 4 servings

Mushroom Enchiladas

Cook under pressure at 15 lbs. for 0 minutes. (See recipe how-to on page 75.)

This is a rich, meatless entrée, full of south-of-the-border flavor. Use more green chilies if you like very, very spicy Mexican food.

3 tablespoons butter or margarine
4 cups thickly-sliced fresh mushrooms
4 ounces canned, diced green chilies, drained
1 cup chopped Bermuda onion
1 package (3 ounces) cream or Neufchatel cheese, cubed
1 cup plain yogurt
3 tablespoons all-purpose flour
½ cup water
3 cups tomato-base enchilada sauce (canned or homemade)
12 corn tortillas
2 cups shredded sharp Cheddar cheese

1. Melt butter in cooker; sauté mushrooms until golden. Stir in chilies, onion, cream cheese, yogurt, and flour.

2. Cook over low heat, stirring until cheese melts and mixture is creamy and bubbling; transfer to bowl.

3. Place rack in cooker; add water. Cut piece of aluminum foil 20 inches long; fit into cooker over rack.

4. Heat enchilada sauce in small saucepan to simmering. Dip a tortilla, using tongs, into simmering enchilada sauce; place tortilla on plate.

5. Spoon 1/12th of cheese mixture on tortilla; roll and place seam-sides-down on foil in cooker. Repeat with 5 tortillas; sprinkle with half the Cheddar cheese.

6. Dip, fill and roll remaining tortillas; place them in a layer on top of tortillas in cooker. Pour 1½ cups enchilada sauce over tortillas; sprinkle with remaining Cheddar cheese. Fold foil around tortillas, leaving top open.

7. Cover and set control at 15. Cook over high heat until pressure is reached. Cook 0 minutes. Remove cooker from heat.

8. Reduce pressure at once by placing cooker under cold, running water. Serve immediately.

Makes 6 servings (2 tortillas each)

Marinated Mushrooms

Cook under pressure at 15 lbs. for 0 minutes.

Marinated fresh mushrooms go well with all kinds of meats. You can also serve them with chicken or tuna salad for lunch or as an appetizer.

¼ cup vegetable oil
1 pound mushrooms, cleaned, trimmed
⅓ cup wine vinegar
1 teaspoon salt
1 teaspoon sugar
½ teaspoon dried basil leaves
⅛ teaspoon pepper
2 tablespoons minced parsley
1 clove garlic, minced
2 tablespoons water
Chopped fresh parsley

1. Heat oil in cooker; sauté mushrooms 1 minute. Stir remaining ingredients except fresh parsley into cooker.

2. Cover and set control at 15. Cook over medium-high heat until pressure is reached. Cook 0 minutes. Remove cooker from heat.

3. Reduce pressure at once by placing cooker under cold, running water.

4. Sprinkle mushrooms with fresh parsley. Refrigerate until chilled.

Makes 8 servings

Meatless Burgers

Cook under pressure at 5 lbs. for 5 minutes (or at 15 lbs. for 2 minutes).

You don't have to be a vegetarian to appreciate this delicious substitute for beef burgers. Serve them on buns for lunch or with a green vegetable for dinner.

2 eggs, slightly beaten
⅔ cup ground mixed nuts
1 cup uncooked rolled oats
¼ cup milk
1 tablespoon minced onion
½ teaspoon salt
½ teaspoon dried basil leaves
2 tablespoons vegetable oil
½ cup warm water

1. Mix eggs, nuts, oats, milk, onion, salt and basil in a medium mixing bowl. Form into 8 patties.

2. Heat oil in cooker; brown patties on both sides over medium-high heat. Remove patties from cooker. Place rack in cooker; pour in water. Place patties on rack making 2 layers if necessary, separating with a round of aluminum foil.

3. Cover and set control at 5. Cook over medium-high heat until pressure is reached. Reduce heat; cook 5 minutes (at 15 pounds pressure, cook 2 minutes).

4. Cool cooker naturally 5 minutes; place cooker under cold, running water to complete pressure reduction.

Makes 4 servings

Spinach Noodle Casserole

Cook under pressure at 15 lbs. for 1 minute, and then 2 minutes more.

The hearty flavor of spinach — or green — noodles stands up well to a tomato sauce seasoned with black olives and topped with sharp Cheddar cheese.

2 quarts water
1 teaspoon salt
½ package (8-ounce size) spinach noodles
1 tablespoon vegetable oil
2 tablespoons butter or margarine
¼ cup instant minced onion
1 cup thinly-sliced mushrooms
1 clove garlic, minced
1 cup tomato sauce
18 ripe, pitted olives, chopped
1 teaspoon salt
⅛ teaspoon pepper
1 cup sharp Cheddar cheese
⅓ cup dry bread crumbs
1 tablespoon butter or margarine
Paprika
¾ cup water

1. Measure 2 quarts water and 1 teaspoon salt into cooker; heat to boiling over high heat. Stir in noodles and oil. Reduce heat to medium.

2. Cover and set control at 15. Cook over medium heat until pressure is reached. Reduce heat; cook 1 minute.

3. Reduce pressure at once by placing cooker under cold, running water. Drain noodles.

4. Heat 2 tablespoons butter in cooker; add onion, mushrooms and garlic; sauté about 1 minute. Remove from heat; stir in tomato sauce, olives, 1 teaspoon salt, the pepper and noodles.

5. Spoon half the noodle mixture into greased 3-cup metal mold. Sprinkle with half the cheese. Repeat layer. Sprinkle with bread crumbs; dot with 1 tablespoon butter. Sprinkle with paprika. Set on rack in cooker; pour in ¾ cup water.

6. Cover and set control at 15. Cook over high heat until pressure is reached. Cook 2 minutes. Remove cooker from heat.

7. Reduce pressure at once by placing cooker under cold, running water.

Makes 3 to 4 servings

Spinach with Rosemary

Cook under pressure at 15 lbs. for 0 minutes.

Spinach retains excellent flavor and texture when cooked in the pressure cooker. Try this recipe garnished with crumbled bacon, if you wish.

1 pound fresh spinach, washed
½ teaspoon dried rosemary
    leaves
¼ teaspoon salt
1 tablespoon minced parsley
1½ teaspoons instant minced
    onion
½ cup water
2 tablespoons butter or
    margarine
1 tablespoon lemon juice

1. Break stems off spinach. Place spinach on rack in cooker. Add rosemary, salt, parsley, onion and water.

2. Cover and set control at 15. Cook over high heat until pressure is reached. Cook 0 minutes. Remove cooker from heat.

3. Reduce pressure at once by placing cooker under cold, running water.

4. Drain excess liquid. Stir in butter and lemon juice.
Makes 3 servings

Creamed Spinach

Cook under pressure at 15 lbs. for 0 minutes.

This is one of our favorite ways to serve spinach. The egg slices are a natural complement and the nutmeg adds a delicate flavor.

1 pound fresh spinach, washed
1 tablespoon finely-chopped
    onion
½ cup water
¼ teaspoon salt
1½ tablespoons butter or
    margarine
1½ tablespoons all-purpose flour
½ cup milk or cream
¼ teaspoon sugar
½ teaspoon salt
⅛ teaspoon white pepper
⅛ teaspoon ground nutmeg
1 hard-cooked egg, sliced

1. Break stems off spinach. Place spinach on rack in cooker. Add onion, water and ¼ teaspoon salt.

2. Cover and set control at 15. Cook over high heat until pressure is reached. Cook 0 minutes. Remove cooker from heat.

3. Reduce pressure at once by placing cooker under cold, running water.

4. Drain and reserve spinach. Heat butter in cooker. Stir in flour to form smooth paste. Cook, stirring occasionally, until flour is brown. Remove from heat. Stir in milk gradually. Cook, stirring constantly, until thickened. Stir in sugar, ½ teaspoon salt, and the pepper; add spinach. Cook over low heat just until spinach is heated.

5. Place spinach in serving bowl. Sprinkle with nutmeg; garnish with egg slices.
Makes 3 servings

Tips:
Always check the vent tube by holding the cover up to the light before using pressure cooker; light should be visible through the tube.

Vegetables that require the same amount of cooking time may be cooked together; flavors will not mingle.

Noodles and Cheese

Cook under pressure at 15 lbs. for 1 minute, and then 8 minutes more.

These creamy noodles make a good, quick lunch entrée on busy days — kids love them. They're equally good served as a side dish with all kinds of meat.

6 ounces broad egg noodles
2 quarts water
1 teaspoon salt
1 tablespoon vegetable oil
1 teaspoon salt
⅛ teaspoon white pepper
1 cup ricotta cheese
4 ounces mozzarella cheese, cut into ¼-inch cubes
1 teaspoon minced onion
¼ teaspoon ground nutmeg
1 egg, slightly beaten
1 cup warm milk
2 cups hot water

1. Place noodles, 2 quarts water, 1 teaspoon salt and 1 tablespoon oil in cooker; heat to boiling.

2. Cover and set control at 15. Cook over medium heat until pressure is reached. Reduce heat; cook 1 minute.

3. Reduce pressure at once by placing cooker under cold, running water. Drain noodles. Rinse out cooker; wipe dry.

4. Mix noodles, 1 teaspoon salt, the pepper, cheeses, onion and nutmeg. Mix egg and milk and add to noodle mixture. Spoon noodle mixture into greased 1-quart mold. Cover mold with double thickness aluminum foil; tie with string to hold foil in place. Place rack in cooker; pour in 2 cups water. Place mold on rack.

5. Cover and set control at 15. Cook over high heat until pressure is reached. Reduce heat; cook 8 minutes.

6. Reduce pressure at once by placing cooker under cold, running water. Let noodles cool 5 to 10 minutes before serving.

Makes 4 servings

Spiced Acorn Squash

Cook under pressure at 15 lbs. for 6 to 7 minutes.

Pressure cooking produces marvelous texture and a buttery, spicy filling enhances the warm flavor of this delicious winter vegetable.

2 medium acorn squash
¼ teaspoon ground cinnamon
1 teaspoon salt
¼ to ½ teaspoon pepper
1 tablespoon brown sugar
1½ teaspoons butter or margarine
8 cloves
1 cup hot water

1. Cut squash in half lengthwise. Scoop out seeds. Mix remaining ingredients, except cloves and water. Spoon into cavity of each squash.

2. Press clove in end of each squash half. Place squash on rack in cooker. Pour in water.

3. Cover and set control at 15. Cook over high heat until pressure is reached. Reduce heat; cook 6 to 7 minutes.

4. Reduce pressure at once by placing cooker under cold, running water.

Makes 4 servings

Macaroni-Cheese-Olive Casserole

Cook under pressure at 15 lbs. for 1 minute, and then 2 minutes more.

Macaroni cooks quickly in the pressure cooker; this tasty, cheese-rich dish is ready to serve in minutes.

1 cup elbow macaroni
1 quart water
1 teaspoon salt
1 tablespoon vegetable oil
2 cups grated Cheddar cheese
⅓ cup milk
½ cup stuffed Spanish pimento olives, sliced
¼ cup sliced onion
6 tomato slices
¼ teaspoon seasoned salt
½ cup dry bread crumbs
  Paprika
2 teaspoons butter or margarine
1 cup water

1. Place macaroni, 1 quart water, the salt and oil into cooker; heat to boiling. Reduce heat.

2. Cover and set control at 15. Cook over medium heat until pressure is reached. Reduce heat; cook 1 minute.

3. Reduce pressure at once by placing cooker under cold, running water.

4. Drain macaroni. Spoon half the macaroni into lightly-greased, oven-proof casserole. Top with half the cheese, milk, olives, onion and tomato slices. Repeat layer.

5. Sprinkle casserole with seasoned salt, bread crumbs, and paprika. Dot top with butter. Set casserole on rack in cooker; pour in 1 cup water.

6. Cover and set control at 15. Heat over medium heat until pressure is reached. Cook 2 minutes. Remove cooker from heat.

7. Reduce pressure at once by placing cooker under cold, running water.

Makes 4 servings

Oriental Specialty

Cook under pressure at 15 lbs. for 0 minutes.

An unusual harmony of flavors and textures, this colorful melange features Oriental vegetables and mandarin oranges cooked in fruit juices.

2 tablespoons peanut or vegetable oil
½ pound fresh bean sprouts
½ pound fresh mushrooms, sliced
1 can (8 ounces) water chestnuts, drained, sliced
1 cup fresh or frozen peas
1 can (8 ounces) fruit cocktail, undrained
½ can (11 ounce-size) mandarin oranges, drained
1 tablespoon cornstarch
3 tablespoons soy sauce
1 teaspoon lemon juice
1 cup hot cooked long-grain rice
Soy sauce

1. Heat oil in cooker; sauté bean sprouts, mushrooms, and water chestnuts about 1 minute.

2. Stir in peas, fruit cocktail with juice and mandarin oranges.

3. Cover and set control at 15. Cook over high heat until pressure is reached. Cook 0 minutes. Remove cooker from heat.

4. Reduce pressure at once by placing cooker under cold, running water.

5. Mix cornstarch, soy sauce and lemon juice; stir into vegetable mixture in cooker. Cook over medium heat, stirring constantly until thickened, about 2 minutes.

6. Serve over hot rice; pass the soy sauce.

Makes 4 servings

Stuffed Zucchini

Cook under pressure at 15 lbs. for 1 minute.

Zucchini lend themselves well to stuffing, and an aromatic mixture of mushrooms and cheese complements the vegetables' delicate taste.

4 small zucchini, washed
2 tablespoons olive or
    vegetable oil
1 cup minced fresh mushrooms
2 slices soft bread, crusts
    trimmed, soaked in a little
    milk
1 egg
½ teaspoon salt
⅛ teaspoon pepper
¼ teaspoon dried oregano
    leaves
2 tablespoons grated
    Parmesan cheese
    Parmesan cheese, grated
    Paprika
½ cup water

1. Cut zucchini in half; scoop out pulp of halves with apple corer, leaving ¼-inch shell. Reserve pulp.

2. Heat olive oil in cooker; sauté mushrooms 1 minute. Squeeze bread dry. Add bread, zucchini pulp, egg, salt, pepper, oregano and 2 tablespoons cheese to cooker; mix well.

3. Fill zucchini shells with mushroom mixture; sprinkle tops with cheese and paprika. Place rack in cooker; pour in water. Layer zucchini on rack in cooker.

4. Cover and set control at 15. Cook over high heat until pressure is reached. Reduce heat; cook 1 minute.

5. Reduce pressure at once by placing cooker under cold, running water.

6. If additional browning is desired, place zucchini under broiler for 2 to 3 minutes.

Makes 4 to 6 servings

Tip:

Cooking times given for vegetables can only be approximate, since size and age will affect timing. Times given will usually produce slightly crisp green vegetables; you may wish to add one or two minutes to cooking times.

Sweet~Sour Zucchini

Cook under pressure at 15 lbs. for 0 minutes.

The perennial Italian favorite, zucchini, is becoming an American staple, served in almost every conceivable way. Pressure-cooked zucchini retains its superb flavor, texture and color.

2 medium zucchini, pared
1 tablespoon vegetable oil
1 tablespoon wine vinegar
1 teaspoon sugar
½ teaspoon salt
⅛ teaspoon pepper
½ teaspoon dried basil leaves
¼ cup water

1. Cut zucchini lengthwise into ⅜-inch slices.

2. Heat oil in cooker. Sauté zucchini until light brown on all sides.

3. Mix vinegar and sugar; spoon over zucchini. Sprinkle with salt, pepper and basil. Add water.

4. Cover and set control at 15. Cook over high heat until pressure is reached. Cook 0 minutes. Remove cooker from heat.

5. Reduce pressure at once by placing cooker under cold, running water.

Makes 4 servings

Fruits and Desserts

PRESSURE COOKING can supply your sweet tooth with a healthier diet by making it very easy to substitute custards, puddings and fruit desserts for more sugar-laden treats. We have been delighted by the satiny texture of the pressure-steamed custards. And the quality of the puddings and fruit "betty's" recommends them even as company fare.

Custards

We have included a half dozen variations on a basic egg custard in this chapter because they turn out so remarkably delicate and smooth. Not only do they cook in just five minutes, but the fine results are completely predictable because the temperature in the pressure cooker is constant and uniform. The technique we have used every time, with slight variations, is quite simple: Start with hot milk. If the recipe requires that you scald the milk, heat it until a thin skin forms on the surface but don't let it boil; remove the milk from the heat to cool it slightly before adding it to the other ingredients. Beat the other ingredients to blend them and add the milk slowly. Cook the mixture in greased, standard 6-ounce oven-proof glass custard cups tightly covered with foil.

All the custards will cook to perfection in five minutes at 15 pounds pressure in 6-ounce glass cups. If you use metal containers, they will cook in less time; so stop the cooking process at three minutes, reduce pressure immediately, and test for doneness by inserting a knife into the center of the custard. If the knife doesn't come out clean, bring the custards back up to pressure and cook a minute or two longer. If you are using very thick ceramic custard cups, the custards may take longer than five minutes. If the center is still runny, the custard hasn't been cooked long enough and needs another minute or two. An overcooked custard will appear watery and the center will be rubbery — a situation that can't be remedied. So if you're using custard cups different from those specified, play it safe and test for doneness sooner rather than later. You only have to test for doneness the first time you use the custard cups in the pressure cooker; every subsequent batch of custard will cook in exactly the same amount of time you've established.

If you can't fit four 6-ounce custard cups on the rack in your cooker, cook them two at a time. Or, if you have a 4-quart or larger cooker, stack them, using two racks. Because the cups don't weigh very much, you can improvise a second rack by piercing a dozen holes in a round, disposable aluminum pan. Be sure that the improvised rack isn't too wide — there should be 3/4 inch space between the edge of the pan and the sides of the cooker.

Puddings

There are several kinds of puddings in this chapter and each calls for a somewhat different procedure. The richly-flavored Indian Pudding must cool for at least 30 minutes before serving; the cornmeal will continue to absorb the milk and the pudding will stiffen as it cools. The Bread Pudding Deluxe and Brown Rice-Raisin Pudding involve techniques similar to those used for custards. We have had best results with oven-proof glass and ceramic containers, but you may prefer a metal mold for attractive serving. Timing is important with these puddings, but it's easier to control because they cook longer. You can test them for doneness, like the custards, with a knife blade.

Fruits

You can steam-poach fruits beautifully on the rack in the cooker — they retain marvelous texture and flavor. Apples "bake" in minutes and you can flavor them any way you wish by coring them and filling the center with a mixture of butter, sugar and spices. For easy but elegant wine-poached pineapple and pear desserts, see the desserts featured in "Complete Dinners." Among the more elaborate, yet quickly-made, fruit desserts in this chapter, you'll find an excellent Apple Brown Betty and an equally appealing Zucchini-Raisin Betty.

Apricot Almond Custard

Cook under pressure at 15 lbs. for 5 minutes. (See recipe how-to on page 78-79.)

The almonds will float to the top of these elegant custards, making them as pretty as they are pleasing.

2 cups milk
2 eggs
¼ cup sugar
2 tablespoons apricot brandy
⅛ teaspoon salt
¼ cup sliced almonds
1 cup water
Toasted sliced almonds, if desired

1. Scald milk; cool slightly.

2. Combine eggs, sugar, brandy and salt; beat lightly to blend. Gradually add hot milk, stirring constantly.

3. Pour mixture into 4 greased 6-ounce custard cups. Sprinkle about 1 tablespoon of almonds over each cup. Cover tightly with aluminum foil. Place custard cups on rack in cooker. (If using a 4-quart or smaller cooker, cook custards 2 at a time.) Pour in water.

4. Cover and set control at 15. Cook over high heat until pressure is reached. Reduce heat; cook 5 minutes.

5. Reduce pressure at once by placing cooker under cold, running water.

6. Cool custards; refrigerate until serving time. Garnish with toasted almonds, if desired.

Makes 4 servings

Crème de Menthe Custard

Cook under pressure at 15 lbs. for 5 minutes.

The cool, pale color of this minty custard hints at its refreshing taste. You can spoon additional crème de menthe over the custards, if you wish.

¾ cup hot milk
1 tablespoon butter, melted
1 egg, beaten
Dash salt
1 tablespoon honey
2 tablespoons crème de menthe
1 cup hot water

1. Mix hot milk and butter.

2. Mix egg, salt, honey and crème de menthe; gradually add milk mixture.

3. Pour mixture into 2 greased 6-ounce custard cups; cover tightly with aluminum foil. Place on rack in cooker; pour in hot water.

4. Cover and set control at 15. Cook over high heat until pressure is reached. Reduce heat; cook 5 minutes.

5. Reduce pressure at once by placing cooker under cold, running water.

6. Cool custards; refrigerate until serving time.

Makes 2 servings

Tip:
A second cooking rack, ordered from the manufacturer, will allow you to stack custard cups in your pressure cooker. Never fill cooker more than two-thirds or three-fourths full, according to manufacturer's recommendation.

Almond Peaches with Custard Sauce

Cook under pressure at 15 lbs. for 0 to 1 minute.

Peaches poached with almonds is typically Italian, but Americans might well adopt this dessert as more and more of us select fruits, fresh or fancied up a bit, to end a meal.

Custard Sauce (recipe
   follows)
2 ounces toasted, blanched
   almonds, finely chopped
1 tablespoon chopped citron
3 tablespoons powdered sugar
6 large fresh peaches, peeled,
   pitted, cut in half
⅓ cup dry sherry
   Cinnamon (see Preparation)
1½ cups water

1. Make Custard Sauce (recipe follows).
2. Mix almonds, citron and sugar; spoon into cavities of peaches. Spoon sherry over peaches; sprinkle with cinnamon.
3. Place rack in cooker; pour in water. Place peaches in cooker, layering them if necessary.
4. Cover and set control at 15. Cook over high heat until pressure is reached. Reduce heat; cook 0 to 1 minute, depending upon ripeness of fruit.
5. Reduce pressure at once by placing cooker under cold, running water.
6. Serve with Custard Sauce.

Makes 6 servings

Custard Sauce

3 eggs, beaten
⅓ cup packed brown sugar
½ teaspoon salt
3 cups milk, scalded
1 teaspoon vanilla

1. Mix eggs, sugar and salt. Stir milk gradually into egg mixture. Strain.
2. Cook mixture, stirring constantly, over very low heat until thickened. Stir in vanilla. Refrigerate.

Makes 3½ cups sauce

Tips:

For best results, use oven-proof glass or ceramic custard cups or bowls for dessert custards and puddings.

Always check the vent tube by holding the cover up to the light before using pressure cooker; light should be visible through the tube.

Mocha Custard

Cook under pressure at 15 lbs. for 5 minutes.

Blended chocolate and coffee make this a special dessert treat. Chocolate lovers will appreciate its deep, rich flavor.

2 cups milk
2 squares unsweetened choco-late
2 teaspoons instant coffee crystals
2 eggs, lightly beaten
3 tablespoons honey
Dash salt
¼ teaspoon ground cinnamon
1 teaspoon vanilla
1 cup hot water
Whipped cream

1. Heat milk until hot; cut chocolate into small pieces and add to milk. Cook over low heat, stirring constantly, until chocolate is melted. Stir in coffee.

2. Mix eggs, honey, salt, cinnamon and vanilla. Mix ¼ cup of the milk mixture into egg mixture; stir egg mixture slowly into milk mixture.

3. Pour milk mixture into 4 greased 6-ounce custard cups. Cover tightly with aluminum foil. Place custard cups on rack in cooker. (If using a 4-quart or smaller cooker, cook custards 2 at a time.) Pour in hot water.

4. Cover and set control at 15. Cook over high heat until pressure is reached. Reduce heat; cook 5 minutes.

5. Reduce pressure at once by placing cooker under cold, running water.

6. Cool custards; refrigerate until serving time. Garnish with whipped cream.

Makes 4 servings

Egg Nog Custard

Cook under pressure at 15 lbs. for 5 minutes.

You'll associate all the warmth and festivity of the traditional holiday brew with the rich flavor of this custard.

2 cups milk
2 eggs
¼ cup sugar
1 tablespoon brandy or 1 teaspoon brandy extract
1½ teaspoons rum or ½ teaspoon rum extract
½ teaspoon nutmeg
⅛ teaspoon salt
1 cup water

1. Scald milk; cool slightly.

2. Combine eggs, sugar, brandy, rum, nutmeg and salt; beat lightly to blend. Gradually add hot milk, stirring constantly.

3. Pour mixture into 4 greased 6-ounce custard cups; cover tightly with aluminum foil. Place custard cups on rack in cooker. (If using a 4-quart or smaller cooker, cook custards 2 at a time.) Pour in water.

4. Cover and set control at 15. Cook over high heat until pressure is reached. Reduce heat; cook 5 minutes.

5. Reduce pressure at once by placing cooker under cold, running water.

6. Cool custards; refrigerate until serving time.

Makes 4 servings

Orange Caramel Flan

Cook under pressure at 15 lbs. for 5 minutes.

A caramel glaze distinguishes this Spanish-style dessert from other custards. The scent of oranges makes it absolutely heavenly!

¼ cup sugar
1 teaspoon grated orange peel
2 cups milk
2 eggs
¼ cup sugar
1 tablespoon orange-flavored liqueur
⅛ teaspoon salt
1 cup water

1. In small, heavy saucepan, combine ¼ cup sugar and orange peel. Cook, stirring constantly, over low heat until the sugar turns into a golden liquid. Remove from heat immediately. Divide syrup among 4 greased 6-ounce custard cups.

2. Scald milk; cool slightly.

3. Combine eggs, ¼ cup sugar, the liqueur and salt; beat lightly to blend. Gradually add hot milk, stirring constantly.

4. Pour mixture into custard cups. Cover tightly with aluminum foil. Place custard cups on rack in cooker. (If using a 4-quart or smaller cooker, cook custards 2 at a time.) Pour in water.

5. Cover and set control at 15. Cook over high heat until pressure is reached. Reduce heat; cook 5 minutes.

6. Reduce pressure at once by placing cooker under cold, running water.

7. Cool custards slightly; unmold on serving plates. Refrigerate.

Makes 4 servings

Lemon Custard

Cook under pressure at 15 lbs. for 5 minutes.

Very lemony, light and delicious, this custard is the perfect ending for a big dinner that everyone will enjoy.

2 cups milk
2 eggs
¼ cup sugar
1 teaspoon lemon extract
½ teaspoon grated lemon peel
⅛ teaspoon salt
1 cup water

1. Scald milk; cool slightly.

2. Combine eggs, sugar, lemon extract, peel and salt; beat lightly to blend. Gradually add hot milk to egg mixture, stirring constantly.

3. Pour mixture into 4 greased 6-ounce custard cups. Cover tightly with aluminum foil. Place custard cups on rack in cooker. (If using 4-quart or smaller cooker, cook custards 2 at a time.) Pour in water.

4. Cover and set control at 15. Cook over high heat until pressure is reached. Reduce heat; cook 5 minutes.

5. Reduce pressure at once by placing cooker under cold, running water.

6. Cool custards; refrigerate until serving time.

Makes 4 servings

Indian Pudding

Cook under pressure at 15 lbs. for 15 minutes.

Corn and molasses make this colonial American classic ever-popular. The pudding stiffens as it cools, so be sure to allow time before serving.

3 cups milk
¾ cup yellow corn meal
1 cup milk
⅓ cup molasses
½ cup sugar
1 teaspoon cinnamon
½ teaspoon ginger
1 teaspoon salt
2 cups water
Whipped cream

1. Heat 3 cups milk to boiling in medium saucepan. Combine corn meal with 1 cup milk; stir into hot milk. Add molasses, sugar, spices and salt; cook over medium heat until mixture thickens, 2 to 3 minutes.

2. Pour mixture into 1½-quart oven-proof bowl that fits loosely in cooker. Cover tightly with aluminum foil. Place rack in cooker; pour in water. Place bowl on rack.

3. Cover and set control at 15. Cook over high heat until pressure is reached. Reduce heat; cook 15 minutes.

4. Reduce pressure at once by placing cooker under cold, running water.

5. Let pudding cool 30 to 45 minutes before serving; serve with whipped cream.

Makes 6 to 8 servings

Bread Pudding Deluxe

Cook under pressure at 15 lbs. for 12 minutes.

Wheat bread and golden raisins enrich this old fashioned favorite. Try it with a drizzling of maple syrup or cream.

2 cups cubed stale wheat bread, crusts removed
½ cup golden raisins
2 tablespoons sugar
⅛ teaspoon salt
½ teaspoon ground cinnamon
2 cups milk
2 eggs, slightly beaten
1 teaspoon vanilla
2 cups water
Cream or maple syrup

1. Mix bread cubes, raisins, sugar, salt and cinnamon in medium bowl.

2. Scald milk in top of double boiler or in metal bowl placed over hot water. Add eggs; cook 2 minutes, stirring constantly. Add vanilla and pour over bread cube mixture.

3. Pour mixture into greased 1-quart mold or oven-proof casserole. Cover with foil; tie with string to hold in place. Place rack in cooker; pour in water. Place mold on rack.

4. Cover and set control at 15. Cook over high heat until pressure is reached. Reduce heat; cook 12 minutes.

5. Reduce pressure at once by placing cooker under cold, running water.

6. Place pudding under broiler to brown and crisp top, if desired. Serve plain, or with cream or maple syrup.

Makes 4 to 6 servings

Brown Rice~Raisin Pudding

Cook under pressure at 15 lbs. for 8 minutes.

This is a creamy, extra nutritious version of plain rice pudding. You can substitute maple flavoring for the vanilla, if you wish.

1½ cups milk
2 eggs, beaten
3 tablespoons honey
Dash salt
1 teaspoon vanilla
Dash cinnamon
1 cup cooked, long-grain
   brown rice
½ cup raisins
1 cup hot water

1. Scald milk; cool slightly.

2. Combine eggs, honey, salt, vanilla and cinnamon. Stir in rice and raisins. Gradually add milk, stirring constantly.

3. Pour mixture into 1-quart mold or oven-proof bowl. Cover with aluminum foil. Place rack in cooker; pour in the hot water. Place mold on rack.

4. Cover and set control at 15. Cook over high heat until pressure is reached. Reduce heat; cook 8 minutes.

5. Cool cooker naturally 5 minutes; place cooker under cold, running water to complete pressure reduction.

6. Stir pudding; cool and refrigerate until cold.

Makes 4 servings

Apple Brown Betty

Cook under pressure at 15 lbs. for 15 minutes.

Incredibly good and easily prepared, this down-home dessert can enhance even a company dinner when served with freshly whipped cream.

½ cup dry bread crumbs
¼ cup brown sugar
1 teaspoon cinnamon
½ teaspoon nutmeg, if desired
1 tablespoon lemon juice
4 cups sliced apples
⅓ cup butter, melted
2 cups water

1. Combine bread crumbs, sugar, spices and lemon juice.

2. In a 1-quart mold or oven-proof bowl, arrange alternate layers of apples and crumb mixture, ending with crumb mixture. Pour melted butter over top. Cover tightly with aluminum foil. Place rack in cooker; pour in water. Place mold on rack.

3. Cover and set control at 15. Cook over high heat until pressure is reached. Reduce heat; cook 15 minutes.

4. Reduce pressure at once by placing cooker under cold, running water.

Makes 4 servings

Tips:

For best results, use oven-proof glass or ceramic custard cups or bowls for dessert custards and puddings.

A second cooking rack, ordered from the manufacturer, will allow you to stack custard cups in your pressure cooker. Never fill cooker more than two-thirds or three-fourths full, according to manufacturer's recommendation.

Zucchini-Raisin Betty

Cook under pressure at 15 lbs. for 15 minutes.

Not only is this dessert nutritious, but it also has a wonderful, not-too-sweet taste. Lemon and spices give it plenty of zest.

2 cups shredded zucchini
1 cup regular rolled oats
1 cup dry bread crumbs
¼ cup packed brown sugar
3 tablespoons lemon juice
1 teaspoon grated lemon rind
1 teaspoon ground cinnamon
⅛ teaspoon ground cloves, if desired
¼ teaspoon ground nutmeg
¼ cup golden raisins
¼ cup shelled sunflower seeds, if desired
¼ cup butter or margarine
2 cups hot water
Cream or whipped cream

1. Mix all ingredients except butter, water and cream.

2. Spoon zucchini mixture into greased 1-quart mold or oven-proof bowl; press mixture lightly to hold in place. Dot top with butter. Cover with two layers of aluminum foil; tie in place with string. Place rack in cooker; pour in hot water. Set mold on rack.

3. Cover and set control at 15. Cook over high heat until pressure is reached. Reduce heat; cook 15 minutes.

4. Reduce pressure at once by placing cooker under cold, running water.

5. Spoon pudding into dessert dishes. Top with cream or whipped cream.

Makes 4 servings

Tip:
Always check the vent tube by holding the cover up to the light before using pressure cooker; light should be visible through the tube.

Hot Buttered Dried Fruits

Soak dried fruits for 30 minutes.

Cook under pressure at 15 lbs. for 2 to 4 minutes.

Any combination of dried fruits may be used for this dessert. They cook well in just a few minutes when soaked for half an hour beforehand.

½ cup dried apricots, chopped
½ cup dried pears, chopped
½ cup dried apples, chopped
3 cups water
1½ cups orange juice
Cinnamon (see Preparation)
¼ cup packed brown sugar
¼ cup toasted slivered almonds
3 tablespoons butter or margarine
1 teaspoon Angostura bitters

1. Soak dried fruits in the water 30 minutes; drain. Place fruits and orange juice in cooker; sprinkle with cinnamon.

2. Cover and set control at 15. Cook over medium heat until pressure is reached. Reduce heat; cook 2 to 4 minutes.

3. Reduce pressure at once by placing cooker under cold, running water.

4. Drain fruits; reserve cooking liquid. Stir brown sugar into fruits.

5. Pour 1 cup cooking liquid into cooker. Add almonds and butter. Simmer, uncovered, 5 minutes. Stir in bitters; pour over fruits.

Makes 4 to 6 servings

Anise Baked Apples

Cook under pressure at 15 lbs. for 7 to 9 minutes.

Vary the spice as you wish in this simple and welcome dessert. You can use ground cinnamon and nutmeg or cardamom and add raisins or chopped nuts.

4 medium baking apples, cored
¼ cup packed brown sugar
1 teaspoon anise seeds,
    crushed
1 cup water
½ cup whipping cream,
    whipped, or plain yogurt

1. Pare 1-inch peel from tops of apples. Mix sugar and anise seeds; spoon into apple cavities, filling to mounded tops. Place each apple on 9-inch square of aluminum foil; bring foil up to form packets, leaving tops open. Set on rack in cooker. Pour in water.

2. Cover and set control at 15. Cook over high heat until pressure is reached. Reduce heat; cook 7 to 9 minutes, depending upon size of apples.

3. Reduce pressure at once by placing cooker under cold, running water.

4. Serve hot or cold with whipped cream or yogurt topping.

Makes 4 servings

Glazed Fruit Peel

Cook under pressure at 15 lbs. for 20 minutes.

This colorful and festive fruit candy is easy to make in a pressure cooker. It takes considerably less time to prepare the grapefruit peel — usually a tedious process.

Peel of 3 grapefruit or 6
    oranges
1 teaspoon salt
    Water (see Preparation)
3 cups sugar
3 drops Angostura bitters
1 cup water
1 cup sugar

1. Remove yellow or orange portion of peel; discard white membrane. Cut peel into strips ¼ inch wide.

2. Place peel and salt in cooker; add water to level of 2 inches from top of cooker.

3. Cover and set control at 15. Cook over high heat until pressure is reached. Reduce heat; cook 20 minutes.

4. Reduce pressure at once by placing cooker under cold, running water.

5. Drain peel on paper toweling.

6. Place 2½ cups sugar, the bitters and 1 cup water in cooker; heat to boiling. Stir in peel; cook, uncovered, stirring often with slotted spoon, until most of syrup has been absorbed.

7. Lift peel with slotted spoon onto wax paper sprinkled with ½ cup of the sugar. Roll to coat completely.

8. Let cool; store in covered containers.

Makes 36 to 40 pieces

Peach Butter

Cook under pressure at 15 lbs. for 5 minutes.

This is a quick and flavorful preserve that is especially great when spread on buttered toast at breakfast.

2 pounds peaches, peeled, pitted
1 cup water
1½ to 2 cups sugar
¼ teaspoon ground cinnamon

1. Place peaches and water in cooker.

2. Cover and set control at 15. Cook over medium heat until pressure is reached. Reduce heat; cook 5 minutes.

3. Reduce pressure at once by placing cooker under cold, running water.

4. Measure peach pulp and return to cooker. Stir in sugar, using ⅔ cup sugar for each cup of fruit. Stir in cinnamon. Boil, uncovered, until thick, stirring often.

5. Pour Peach Butter into hot sterilized glasses or jars, leaving ½-inch space at top. Cover with melted paraffin. Store in cool, dark place.

Makes four 6-ounce glasses

Curried Fruit

Cook under pressure at 15 lbs. for 5 minutes.

A sweet condiment, this fruit medley goes well with ham, pork or poultry. The curry provides a piquant accent for the pineapple, pears and peaches.

½ cup butter or margarine
1 cup packed brown sugar
2½ teaspoons imported Indian curry
¾ pound fresh pineapple, pared, sliced or 1 can (1 pound 4 ounces) pineapple slices, drained
1 pound pears, pared, cored, sliced
1 pound peaches, peeled, pitted, sliced
½ jar (10-ounce size) maraschino cherries, drained
1 cup hot water
Dillweed

1. Melt butter in cooker; stir in sugar and curry. Place fruits in greased 1-quart mold; pour sugar mixture over fruit. Cover mold tightly with aluminum foil.

2. Place rack in cooker; pour in hot water. Place mold on rack.

3. Cover cooker and set control at 15. Cook over high heat until pressure is reached. Reduce heat; cook 5 minutes.

4. Cool cooker naturally 5 minutes; place cooker under cold, running water to complete pressure reduction.

5. Pour mixture into serving bowl. Sprinkle lightly with dillweed. Refrigerate until chilled.

Makes 10 to 12 servings

Breads and Puddings

IF YOU LOOK forward to the annual ritual of steamed Christmas pudding, you can anticipate with equal pleasure the flavors and aromas of the rich, moist steamed puddings in this chapter. The only difference is that these puddings take so little time to cook that we've included some less-elaborate recipes so that you can enjoy the pleasures of steamed puddings year-around. We've also applied the same pressure-cooking techniques in an enticing array of fragrant quick breads.

Steaming Without Pressure

The recipes for both breads and puddings include one important step different from other pressure cooker techniques: These foods must be steamed without pressure for 20 to 30 minutes before they are cooked under pressure. This step encourages the dough to rise and become fluffy. If you were to cook these leavened foods under pressure from the very beginning, the fast heat penetration would impede the action of the baking powder or baking soda. Even in the recipe for Steamed Christmas Pudding, which has no leavening other than egg whites, we steam the pudding without pressure first to prevent sogginess.

To steam without pressure, you simply cover the cooker without setting the control or closing the steam valve. When you heat the cooker, steam should escape from the vent tube in a slow, steady stream. Adjust the heat under the cooker so that the steam neither rushes out nor stops flowing completely. If the steam rushes out too quickly, you face the danger of boiling away all the water in the cooker. If there isn't sufficient steam, the dough won't rise. So watch the steam carefully and adjust the heat under the cooker accordingly. If you suspect that you have allowed too much steam to escape, allow the cooker to cool naturally for a few minutes, open it and add more water.

Steamed Bread And Pudding Containers

We have recommended specific cooking containers in each recipe. For breads, we use tin cans; for puddings, metal molds. Cooking times given in the recipes correspond to the size of these containers. You can use any containers you wish, however, if they will fit in your cooker and allow at least 3/4 inch of space for steam to circulate on all sides. But if you use a different container than that specified, you'll have to adjust cooking times. If your container is larger, the dough will take longer to steam; if it's smaller, the dough will steam faster. If, for example, you want to cook the Boston Brown Bread in two 1 pound, 12-ounce size cans, you can do so. But the bread will take longer to cook and the first time you use the cans, you'll have to gauge the cooking time by trial and error. Don't fill any container more than half full, for the dough must have room to rise.

Filling The Cooker

Always steam breads and puddings on the rack. Make sure there is 3/4-inch of space between the containers and the sides of the cooker and that there is at least two inches of space between the tops of the containers and the rim of the pot. If you can't fit all the cans in your cooker at once, steam only as many at one time as will fit safely. Refrigerate the other cans, covered, until you're ready to steam them.

Testing For Doneness

You can try various cans and containers without fear of ruining a recipe because it's very easy to test for doneness and cook breads and puddings longer, if necessary. To test for doneness, reduce pressure as directed in the recipe. Untie the string and remove the aluminum foil from a can or mold. Insert a knife blade into the bread or pudding; the blade should come out clean. If it doesn't, add at least 1/2 cup water to the water remaining in the cooker; then cover the cooker, bring it back up to pressure, and cook the food longer. The amount of additional cooking time needed will depend on the size of the container.

Old-Fashioned Carrot Pudding

Steam pudding for 20 minutes.

Cook under pressure at 15 lbs. for 40 to 45 minutes.

Carrot pudding is an old-time favorite that's perfect not only for cold, winter nights but for any night when a substantial dessert is desired.

⅔ cup all-purpose flour
⅓ cup sugar
1 teaspoon baking powder
½ teaspoon salt
½ teaspoon baking soda
1 teaspoon ground allspice
1 cup raisins
1 cup shredded carrot
1 small potato, pared, shredded
⅓ cup honey
⅓ cup milk
4 cups water

1. Mix all ingredients except honey, milk and water. Add honey and milk; stir just until all ingredients are moistened.

2. Pour mixture into greased 4-cup metal mold or oven-proof casserole. Cover with a double layer of aluminum foil; tie foil in place with string. Pour water into cooker. Place mold on rack in cooker.

3. Cover cooker, but do not set control. Cook over medium heat for 20 minutes, allowing steam to escape from vent.

4. Set control at 15. Cook over high heat until pressure is reached. Reduce heat; cook 40 to 45 minutes.

5. Reduce pressure at once by placing cooker under cold, running water.

6. Serve hot with Custard or Hard Sauce (see Index).
Makes 4 servings

Boston Brown Bread

Steam bread for 30 minutes. (See recipe how-to on pages 77-78.)

Cook under pressure at 5 lbs. for 30 minutes (or at 15 lbs. for 16 minutes).

This is an easy nutritious bread that can add richness to a simple lunch or supper.

2 eggs, well beaten
2 tablespoons butter or margarine, melted
⅔ cup dark molasses
1 teaspoon baking soda
1 cup buttermilk
1 cup all-purpose flour
1 cup graham flour
1 cup rye flour
1 teaspoon baking powder
½ teaspoon salt
½ cup golden raisins
½ cup chopped nuts
3 cups hot water

1. Mix eggs, butter and molasses. Stir baking soda into buttermilk; reserve.

2. Combine flours with baking powder and salt. Stir buttermilk and flour mixtures into egg mixture alternately. Stir in raisins and nuts.

3. Fill 3 or 4 greased tin cans (1 pound, 4 ounce size, or smaller) one-half full. Cover with double thickness of aluminum foil; tie with string to hold in place. Place cans on rack in cooker. (If your cooker cannot hold all 4 cans with ¾-inch space between cans and sides of cooker, steam cans 2 at a time.) Pour hot water into cooker.

4. Cover cooker, but do not set control. Cook over medium heat for 30 minutes, allowing steam to escape from vent.

5. Set control at 5. Cook over high heat until pressure is reached. Reduce heat; cook 30 minutes (at 15 pounds pressure, cook 16 minutes).

6. Reduce pressure at once by placing cooker under cold, running water. *Makes about 32 slices*

Apricot~Herb Bread

Simmer fruit for 10 minutes. Steam bread for 30 minutes.

Cook under pressure at 5 lbs. for 25 minutes (or at 15 lbs. for 15 minutes).

A touch of rosemary complements the natural flavor of apricots in this molasses-sweetened bread.

1 cup chopped dried apricots or pitted prunes
1½ cups water
1½ teaspoons dried rosemary leaves
2 tablespoons vegetable shortening
½ cup dark molasses
1 egg
1½ cups all-purpose flour
1 teaspoon salt
1 teaspoon baking soda
3 cups hot water

1. Place fruit, water and rosemary in cooker; heat to boiling. Reduce heat; simmer 10 minutes. Drain; reserve ½ cup cooking liquid.

2. Mix shortening, molasses and egg; mix with fruit and reserved liquid.

3. Stir flour, salt and soda into fruit mixture. Spoon batter into 4 greased 10¾-ounce cans. Cover with aluminum foil and tie with string to hold in place. Place cans on rack in cooker. (If your cooker cannot hold all 4 cans with ¾-inch space between cans and sides, steam cans 2 at a time.) Pour in hot water.

4. Cover cooker, but do not set control. Cook over medium heat for 30 minutes, allowing steam to escape from vent.

5. Set control at 5. Cook over high heat until pressure is reached. Reduce heat; cook 25 minutes (at 15 pounds pressure, cook 15 minutes).

6. Reduce pressure at once by placing cooker under cold, running water.

7. Let cans stand 10 minutes; place cans on rack to complete cooling. *Makes about 28 slices*

Banana~Prune Bread

Steam bread for 30 minutes.

Cook under pressure at 5 lbs. for 30 minutes (or at 15 lbs. for 16 minutes).

Another of those good fruited breads that steam well, this recipe combines bananas and prunes for interesting texture and doubly rich taste.

¾ cup sugar
⅓ cup vegetable shortening
2 eggs
1 cup mashed bananas
2 cups all-purpose flour
¾ teaspoon salt
2 teaspoons baking powder
¼ teaspoon ground allspice
¼ teaspoon baking soda
½ cup finely-chopped prunes
3 cups hot water

1. Cream sugar and shortening in large mixing bowl. Beat in eggs one at a time, until smooth. Stir in bananas.

2. Combine flour, salt, baking powder, allspice and baking soda; stir into creamed mixture in two additions, beating until smooth after each addition. Fold in prunes.

3. Spoon batter into 4 greased cans (10¾-ounce size). Cover with aluminum foil; tie with string to hold in place. Place cans on rack in cooker. (If your cooker cannot hold all 4 cans with ¾-inch space between

Banana-Prune Bread (Continued)

cans and sides of cooker, steam cans 2 at a time.) Pour in hot water.

4. Cover cooker, but do not set control. Cook over medium heat for 30 minutes, allowing steam to escape from vent.

5. Set control at 5. Cook over medium heat until pressure is reached. Reduce heat; cook 30 minutes (at 15 pounds pressure, cook 16 minutes).

6. Reduce pressure at once by placing cooker under cold, running water.

7. Let cans stand 10 minutes; place on rack to complete cooling.

Makes about 28 slices

Tip:

Be sure to allow at least three-fourths inch of space for steam to circulate around cans or metal molds. Always reduce heat once pressure has been reached.

Raisin-Bran Bread

Steam bread for 30 minutes.

Cook under pressure at 5 lbs. for 30 minutes (or at 15 lbs. for 16 minutes).

Made with all-bran, raisins, currants and nuts, this bread could be made the night before and served with butter the next morning for breakfast.

1 egg, beaten
2 tablespoons butter or margarine, melted
⅓ cup dark molasses
1 teaspoon baking soda
1 cup buttermilk
1½ cups all-purpose flour
1 teaspoon baking powder
½ teaspoon salt
1¼ cups all-bran cereal
½ cup currants
½ cup golden raisins
½ cup chopped walnuts
3 cups hot water

1. Mix egg, butter and molasses. Stir baking soda into buttermilk. Combine flour, baking powder, salt and cereal. Stir buttermilk and flour mixtures alternately into egg mixture. Stir in currants, raisins and nuts.

2. Spoon batter into 4 greased cans (10¾-ounce size). Cover cans with foil; tie with string to hold in place.

3. Place cans on rack in cooker. (If your cooker cannot hold all 4 cans with ¾-inch space between cans and sides of cooker, steam 2 cans at a time.) Pour in hot water.

4. Cover cooker, but do not set control. Cook over medium heat for 30 minutes, allowing steam to escape from vent.

5. Set control at 5. Cook over high heat until pressure is reached. Reduce heat; cook 30 minutes (at 15 pounds pressure, cook 16 minutes).

6. Reduce pressure at once by placing cooker under cold, running water.

7. Let cans stand 10 minutes; place on rack to complete cooling.

Makes about 32 slices

Peach Nut Bread

Steam bread for 30 minutes.

Cook under pressure at 5 lbs. for 30 minutes (or at 15 lbs. for 16 minutes).

Fresh peaches make this bread moist and unusually good. You can substitute apples when peaches are not available.

2 cups all-purpose flour
4 teaspoons baking powder
1 teaspoon salt
⅔ cup sugar
½ cup chopped pecans
¾ cup uncooked peaches, finely chopped
1 egg, slightly beaten
1 cup milk
2 tablespoons butter or margarine, melted
3 cups hot water

1. Combine flour, baking powder, salt and sugar; stir in pecans and peaches.

2. Mix egg, milk and butter. Add to dry ingredients, stirring just until flour is moistened.

3. Spoon batter into 4 greased cans (10¾-ounce size). Cover with aluminum foil; tie with string to hold in place.

4. Allow to stand 20 minutes, then place on rack in cooker. (If your cooker cannot hold all four cans with ¾-inch space between cans and sides of cooker, steam cans 2 at a time.) Pour in hot water.

5. Cover cooker, but do not set control. Cook over medium heat for 30 minutes, allowing steam to escape from vent.

6. Set control at 5. Cook over high heat until pressure is reached. Reduce heat; cook 30 minutes (at 15 pounds pressure, cook 16 minutes).

7. Reduce pressure at once by placing cooker under cold, running water.

8. Remove foil; let cans stand 10 minutes. Place cans on rack to complete cooling.

Makes about 28 slices

Steamed Pudding with Hard Sauce

Steam pudding for 20 minutes.

Cook under pressure at 15 lbs. for 40 minutes.

The fragrance and taste of this moist, cake-like pudding are irresistible. Fruit makes it festive; yet it's simple enough to make for an everyday treat.

Hard Sauce (recipe follows)
½ cup butter or margarine
½ cup packed brown sugar
2 egg yolks, beaten
1 cup all-purpose flour
½ teaspoon baking powder
1 teaspoon ground nutmeg
½ teaspoon ground allspice
Dash salt
2 tablespoons milk
1 tablespoon sherry
¼ cup finely-chopped citron or lemon or orange peel
¼ cup golden raisins
¼ cup chopped candied pineapple
2 tablespoons finely-chopped pitted dates
2 tablespoons finely-chopped maraschino cherries
¼ cup chopped walnuts
4 cups hot water

1. Make Hard Sauce (recipe follows).

2. Beat butter and sugar until light and fluffy. Beat in egg yolks.

3. Mix flour, baking powder, nutmeg, allspice and salt; mix into butter mixture alternately with milk and sherry. Stir in fruits and nuts.

4. Spoon batter into a greased 1-quart mold; cover with aluminum foil and tie in place with string. Pour water into cooker. Place mold on rack in cooker.

5. Cover cooker, but do not set control. Cook over medium heat for 20 minutes, allowing steam to escape from vent.

6. Set control at 15. Cook over high heat until pressure is reached. Reduce heat; cook 40 minutes.

7. Reduce pressure at once by placing cooker under cold, running water. Serve hot with Hard Sauce.

Makes 6 to 8 servings

Hard Sauce

5 tablespoons butter or margarine (room temperature)
1 cup powdered sugar, sifted
⅛ teaspoon salt
1 teaspoon brandy
2 tablespoons cream or milk

1. Beat butter until fluffy; beat in sugar gradually.

2. Mix in salt and brandy.

3. Mix in cream; beat until sauce is smooth. Refrigerate until serving time.

Tips:

Steaming over low heat without pressure allows breads and puddings to rise before cooking; steam should escape through vent pipe in a small, steady stream.

Always check the vent tube by holding the cover up to the light before using pressure cooker; light should be visible through the tube.

Steamed Christmas Pudding

Steam pudding for 20 minutes.

Cook under pressure at 5 lbs. for 60 minutes (or at 15 lbs. for 40 minutes).

Old-time custom favors the early making of Christmas puddings, which keep well when wrapped in aluminum foil until Christmas Day.

½ cup finely-chopped or ground suet
½ pound golden raisins
½ pound currants
½ cup whole wheat flour
1 teaspoon ground cinnamon
¼ teaspoon ground mace
½ teaspoon ground allspice
⅛ teaspoon ground nutmeg
½ teaspoon salt
3 tablespoons sugar
1 apple, cored, chopped
¼ pound finely-chopped mixed glazed fruits
4 eggs, separated
2 tablespoons cream
2 tablespoons sherry
2 tablespoons rum
1½ cups dry bread crumbs
4 cups boiling water

1. Coat suet, raisins and currants with flour. Mix any unused flour with spices, salt, sugar and apple; mix in glazed fruits, suet, raisins and currants. Stir in egg yolks, cream, sherry, rum and bread crumbs.

2. Beat egg whites until stiff, but not dry, peaks form. Fold into flour mixture. (Do final mixing with hands if mixture is too stiff to mix with spoon.)

3. Pour batter into 2 greased 4-cup metal molds. (You will have to cook puddings one at a time.) Cover with double thickness of aluminum foil; tie with string to hold in place. Place one mold on rack in cooker; pour in water.

4. Cover cooker, but do not set control. Cook over medium heat for 20 minutes, allowing steam to escape from vent.

5. Set control at 5. Cook over high heat until pressure is reached. Reduce heat; cook 60 minutes (at 15 pounds pressure, cook 40 minutes).

6. Reduce pressure instantly by placing cooker under cold, running water.

Makes 2 puddings, about 12 servings

Complete Dinners

YOU CAN DOUBLE and triple the speedy convenience of pressure cooking by cooking several foods at the same time. You can do this with virtually any foods that will cook in the same length of time as long as you don't fill the cooker more than two-thirds or three-fourths full, according to the manufacturer's recommendations. To showcase this special feature of pressure cooking, we've created whole dinner menus that cook in only three to twelve minutes. Each menu yields one or two servings of several courses. If your cooker is large enough, you can increase amounts without increasing cooking times. Regardless of quantities or number of meal courses you cook together, you'll only have one pot to wash afterwards.

The Secret Is Timing

Everything in each of these menus cooks under pressure in the same amount of time. So you don't have to remove the cooker and reduce pressure in order to add ingredients in a sequence of different times.

There are a few tricks to coordinating timing. And if you follow these, you can change ingredients in our dinners and create your own menus too. It's easiest to begin with the cooking time of one food and adjust the other foods to match. You can adjust cooking times in these ways:

1) By cutting foods into varying sizes and thicknesses. For example, a 1-inch thick, 4-ounce piece of round steak takes about 13 minutes to cook. Small whole carrots take only about two minutes to cook. Buf if you cut the steak into thin slices and use large rather than small carrots, you can cook the two foods in the same amount of time because it's the depth and diameter of the food rather than total weight or volume that determines cooking time.

2) By wrapping foods in aluminum foil. For example, a 1-1/2-inch cube of beef requires at least five minutes to cook. Fresh Brussels sprouts take only three minutes to cook. But

you can wrap the Brussels sprouts in foil and increase their cooking time so that both foods can cook together.

3) By browning meat and poultry in butter or vegetable oil in the open cooker before adding ingredients that require less time to cook.

4) By using marinades to pre-tenderize — and add flavor to — meats, so that they require less time to cook.

You can "mix and match" any foods from the menus in this chapter that require the same cooking time. The Beef Kabobs Dinner, Lamb Chop Dinner, Cornish Hen Dinner, Pork Chop Dinner and Salmon Dinner all cook in five minutes at 15 pounds pressure. So you can mix the meat from one of these menus with the vegetables from another and the dessert from a third and cook the "new" menu in five minutes. Use the largest amount of water specified for one of these menus. Pressure is reduced the same way in all these menus.

You can also prepare any single item from any menu separately; use the same amount of water, the same cooking time and the same method of pressure reduction required for the whole menu.

Arranging Food In The Cooker

Because everything in the pressure cooker cooks at the same rate, the arrangement of the food in the cooker does not affect cooking times. Our directions for placing food in the cooker are based on convenience. For convenience as well, as we always place the rack in the cooker and add the water before arranging the food on the rack. The only hard and fast rule is that the cooker not be filled more than two-thirds or three-fourths full, according to the manufacturer's directions.

The menus in this chapter will allow you the unique pleasure of preparing and serving complete homemade meals in far less time, and with very little more effort, than it takes to go out to eat. So you can economize, relax and enjoy dinner at home all at the same time.

Beef Kabobs Dinner

Marinate meat for 30 minutes before cooking.

Cook under pressure at 15 lbs. for 5 minutes.

There is a marvelous harmony of tangy and sweet flavors in this dinner. We especially like the combination of fresh pineapple and Oriental plum wine, but you can substitute another sweet wine, or orange or pineapple juice. If you have only large carrots, cut them in half and they'll cook in the same amount of time.

Beef Kabobs

½ cup dry red wine
1 tablespoon red wine vinegar
1 teaspoon Worcestershire sauce
1 teaspoon salt
¼ teaspoon pepper
¾ pound beef sirloin, cut into 1½-inch chunks
½ cup water
2 medium onions, peeled
1 green pepper

Buttered Carrots

6 small whole carrots, trimmed, scraped
½ teaspoon salt
1 tablespoon butter or margarine

Pineapple in Plum Wine

2 slices fresh pineapple, cut 1-inch thick each
½ cup plum wine

1. Combine wine, vinegar, Worcestershire sauce, 1 teaspoon salt and the pepper. Marinate beef in wine mixture at least 30 minutes. Drain meat and reserve marinade. Place rack and water in cooker.

2. Cut onions in thirds. Cut green pepper into 8 pieces. Thread meat and vegetables onto three or four 8-inch skewers; place on rack in cooker. Pour reserved marinade over skewers.

3. Place carrots on square of aluminum foil; sprinkle with ½ teaspoon salt and dot with butter. Fold up corners of foil to form packet. Place over skewers in cooker.

4. Peel pineapple and cut out center core. Place slices in center of 12-inch square of foil. Fold up corners of foil to form packet, leaving top open. Pour wine in center of pineapple. Place packet on rack in cooker alongside skewers.

5. Cover and set control at 15. Cook over high heat until pressure is reached. Reduce heat; cook 5 minutes.

6. Cool cooker naturally 5 minutes; place cooker under cold, running water to complete pressure reduction.

7. Place pineapple rings in individual serving dishes; pour wine from packet over each.

8. Remove beef kebabs and carrot packet from cooker. Serve meat and vegetables over bed of rice, if desired.

Makes 2 servings

Tips:

You may stack foods in the pressure cooker, using additional racks if necessary, but never fill cooker more than two-thirds or three-fourths full, according to manufacturer's recommendation.

Any of the foods in the dinner menu recipes may be prepared separately; use the same amount of water specified for the whole menu. Any foods that require the same cooking time may be prepared together; use the largest amount of water specified for a complete menu. Always reduce heat once pressure has been reached.

Lamb Chop Dinner

Cook under pressure at 15 lbs. for 5 minutes.

This menu shows off pressure cooking to advantage in three ways: The shoulder lamb chops come out very juicy and flavorful (you can substitute ½-inch thick pork chops, if you wish). The squash retains excellent texture and doesn't dry out. And the pears are delicately sweet and succulent.

Lamb Chops

    2 shoulder lamb chops, ½-inch
        thick
    ½ teaspoon salt
    ½ teaspoon crushed basil
    ⅛ teaspoon black pepper
    1 tablespoon vegetable oil
    1 cup water

Acorn Squash

    1 small acorn squash
        Salt
        Pepper

Poached Pears

    2 pears
    1 cup water
    ½ cup sugar
    ¼ cup Port wine

1. Sprinkle lamb chops with ½ teaspoon salt, the basil and ⅛ teaspoon pepper. Heat oil in bottom of cooker. Brown chops on both sides; remove from cooker. Place rack and water in cooker. Place chops on square of aluminum foil. Fold up corners of foil to form packet, leaving top open.

2. Cut squash in half; scoop out seeds. Sprinkle squash with salt and pepper to taste.

3. Pare and core pears. Place pears in center of 8-inch square of foil. Fold up corners of foil to form packet, leaving top open. In small saucepan, combine water and sugar. Stir over medium heat until sugar is dissolved. Pour half the sugar syrup over each pear.

4. Place pear packet on rack in cooker. Arrange squash halves on rack. Place lamb chop packet over squash.

5. Cover and set control at 15. Cook over high heat until pressure is reached. Reduce heat; cook 5 minutes.

6. Cool cooker naturally 5 minutes; place cooker under cold, running water to complete pressure reduction.

7. Place pears in individual serving dishes; pour 2 tablespoons of Port wine over each.

Makes 2 servings

Meatball Dinner

Cook under pressure at 15 lbs. for 12 minutes. (See recipe how-to on page 77.)

Mushrooms and green pepper add much flavor to the ground beef in this menu. We wrap the stuffed apple in aluminum foil so that it cooks more slowly and will not be overdone when the meatball and artichoke are ready. Pressure-cooked artichokes retain better texture and flavor than those cooked conventionally, and you save time too!

Mushroom-Stuffed Meatball

   1 tablespoon dry bread crumbs
   1 tablespoon milk
   ¼ teaspoon salt
     Dash pepper
   ½ teaspoon minced onion
   3 mushrooms, finely chopped
   2 tablespoons chopped green pepper, if desired
   ⅓ pound ground beef
   1 tablespoon vegetable oil
   1 cup water

Artichoke with Mayonnaise

   1 medium artichoke
   ½ teaspoon salt
   2 teaspoons instant minced onion
   ¼ cup mayonnaise or salad dressing

Baked Stuffed Apple

   1 large apple
   1 teaspoon raisins
   1 teaspoon brown sugar
   ½ teaspoon butter or margarine
     Cinnamon (see Preparation)
   1 lemon slice

1. Mix bread crumbs, milk, ¼ teaspoon salt, the pepper, ½ teaspoon onion, mushrooms, green pepper and beef. Form into meatball.

2. Heat oil in cooker; cook meatball until brown on all sides. Remove meatball. Place water and rack in cooker. Place meatball on rack.

3. Cut off artichoke stem one-half inch from top; trim leaves. Place artichoke on rack in cooker; sprinkle with ½ teaspoon salt. Mix 2 tablespoons onion and the mayonnaise; refrigerate until serving time.

4. Core apple; fill cavity with mixture of raisins, sugar and ½ teaspoon butter. Sprinkle apple with cinnamon; top with lemon slice. Place apple on large square of aluminum foil; fold up corners of foil to form packet, leaving top open. Place on rack.

5. Cover and set control at 15. Cook over high heat until pressure is reached. Reduce heat; cook 12 minutes.

6. Cool cooker naturally 5 minutes; place cooker under cold, running water to complete pressure reduction.

Makes 1 serving

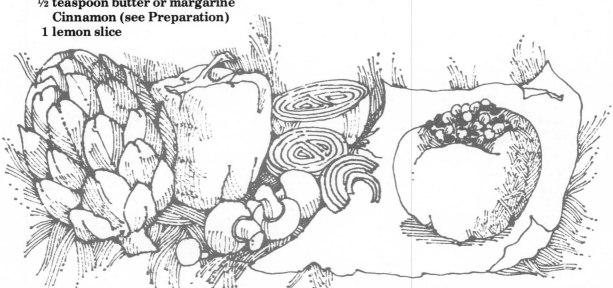

Meat Loaf Dinner

Cook under pressure at 15 lbs. for 10 minutes.

These are fluffy, savory meat loaves that go well with the fruit flavor of the mashed sweet potatoes. We wrap the carrots and celery tightly in aluminum foil and cook them whole so that they don't overcook. You can prepare a sweet potato half without over-cooking, in the same time if you place it in a foil packet, leaving the top open.

Mini Meat Loaves

⅔ **pound ground beef**
1 **egg**
⅓ **cup bread crumbs**
2 **tablespoons catsup**
1 **tablespoon instant minced onion**
1 **small garlic clove, minced**
⅛ **teaspoon ground allspice**
⅛ **teaspoon ground thyme**
1 **tablespoon vegetable oil**
1 **cup water**

Mashed Sweet Potatoes In Orange Juice

1 **large sweet potato, peeled**
¼ **cup or more orange juice**
2 **teaspoons butter or margarine**

Carrots and Celery

2 **large carrots, trimmed, scraped**
1 **stalk celery, trimmed**
1 **tablespoon butter or margarine**
1 **tablespoon minced parsley**

1. Mix beef, egg, bread crumbs, catsup, onion, garlic, allspice and thyme. Shape mixture into 2 flat loaves. Brown loaves on both sides in oil. Remove loaves. Place rack and water in cooker. Place loaves on rack.

2. Place sweet potato on rack in cooker.

3. Place carrots and celery on 12-inch square of aluminum foil; wrap securely. Place on top of potato.

4. Cover and set control at 15. Cook over high heat until pressure is reached. Reduce heat; cook 10 minutes.

5. Reduce pressure at once by placing cooker under cold, running water.

6. Mash potato with orange juice and 2 teaspoons butter. Slice carrots and celery and season with 1 tablespoon butter and the parsley.

Makes 2 servings

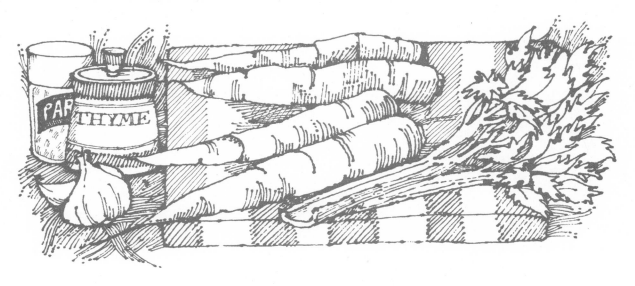

Cornish Hen Dinner

Cook under pressure at 15 lbs. for 5 minutes.

We appreciate the speed with which a Cornish hen cooks tender and juicy in the pressure cooker. If you're using a frozen hen, be sure it's completely thawed before cooking. You can substitute chicken breasts in this recipe, if you wish, and stack them in the cooker, if necessary. The rice pudding is truly a treat — served warm or chilled.

Cornish Hen

    1 Cornish hen, cut in half
    1 teaspoon salt
    ½ teaspoon crushed tarragon
    ¼ teaspoon white pepper
    2 tablespoons vegetable oil
    1 cup water

Mushrooms and Onions

    ¼ pound button mushrooms
    8 small whole onions or 2
        medium onions
    Salt
    Pepper
    1 tablespoon butter or
        margarine

Rice Pudding

    1 cup milk
    1 egg
    ¼ cup sugar
    ½ teaspoon vanilla extract
    ⅛ teaspoon salt
    ⅔ cup cooked rice

1. Rinse Cornish hen halves with cold water; towel dry. Sprinkle halves with 1 teaspoon salt, the tarragon and pepper. Heat oil in bottom of cooker. Brown halves on both sides; remove from cooker. Place rack and water in cooker. Place halves on rack.

2. Clean mushrooms; peel onions. If using medium onions, quarter. Place mushrooms and onions in center of 12-inch square of aluminum foil. Sprinkle with salt and pepper; place butter on top. Fold up corners of foil to form packet.

3. Scald milk for pudding in small saucepan; cool slightly and reserve. Combine egg, sugar, vanilla and ⅛ teaspoon salt in mixing bowl; beat lightly to blend. Stir in rice. Gradually add milk, stirring constantly. Pour into small, oven-proof bowl; cover tightly with foil.

4. Place bowl on rack. Place vegetable packet in cooker over hen.

5. Cover and set control at 15. Cook over high heat until pressure is reached. Reduce heat; cook 5 minutes.

6. Cool cooker naturally 5 minutes; place cooker under cold, running water to complete pressure reduction.

Makes 1 to 2 servings

Pork Chop Dinner

Marinate meat 6 to 12 hours before cooking.

Cook under pressure at 15 lbs. for 5 minutes.

A spicy marinade adds excitement to pork chops. And canned soup allows you to make savory scalloped potatoes in minutes. The pressure cooker works wonders, however, with the beets — both in cutting down on cooking time and in preserving vitamins.

Hawaiian Pork Chops

2 pork chops, ½-inch thick each
1 tablespoon vegetable oil
1 tablespoon catsup
1½ teaspoons soy sauce
1 tablespoon brown sugar
½ teaspoon dried dillweed
1 tablespoon vegetable oil
2 slices pineapple
1 cup water

Scalloped Potatoes

2 medium potatoes, pared, thinly sliced
2 teaspoons instant minced onion
1 teaspoon butter or margarine
1 teaspoon salt
Dash white pepper
1 can (10½ ounces) cheese soup
⅛ teaspoon dried dillweed
Paprika

Small Whole Beets

4 small beets, pared
¼ teaspoon salt
½ tablespoon arrowroot
2 tablespoons orange juice
½ tablespoon honey
1 tablespoon cider vinegar

1. Brush chops with mixture of 1 tablespoon oil, the catsup, soy sauce, brown sugar and ½ teaspoon dillweed. Refrigerate 6 hours or overnight, turning occasionally.

2. Heat 1 tablespoon oil in cooker; brown chops in oil on both sides. Top with pineapple slices. Remove chops. Place rack and water in cooker. Stack chops on rack.

3. Place half of potatoes on 12-inch square of aluminum foil; top with 1 teaspoon onion, ½ teaspoon butter, ½ teaspoon salt and the pepper. Spoon half the cheese soup over potatoes; repeat layer. Fold up corners of foil to form packet, leaving top open. Sprinkle with ⅛ teaspoon dillweed and the paprika. Place on rack with chops.

4. Slice beets ⅜-inch thick; place on square of foil. Fold up corners of foil to form packet, leaving top open. Sprinkle beets with ¼ teaspoon salt. Place on rack in cooker.

5. Cover and set control at 15. Cook over high heat until pressure is reached. Reduce heat; cook 5 minutes.

6. Cool cooker naturally 5 minutes; place cooker under cold, running water to complete pressure reduction.

7. Remove meat; place chops, potatoes and beets on serving platter.

8. Mix arrowroot, orange juice, honey and vinegar; heat to boiling in small saucepan. Boil 1 minute; spoon over beets.

Makes 1 to 2 servings

Tips:

Any of the foods in the dinner menu recipes may be prepared separately; use the same amount of water specified for the whole menu. Any foods that require the same cooking time may be prepared together; use the largest amount of water specified for a complete menu. Always reduce heat once pressure has been reached.

You may stack foods in the pressure cooker, using additional racks if necessary, but never fill cooker more than two-thirds or three-fourths full, according to manufacturer's recommendation.

Barbecued Sparerib Dinner

Cook under pressure at 15 lbs. for 6 minutes.

You save a great deal of time cooking spareribs this way. Use any barbecue sauce you wish, and, if the ribs are extra large, cut them into two-rib pieces before cooking. Pressure cooking produces the best corn on the cob we've ever tasted! And the Brussels sprouts turn out just slightly crunchy and delicious.

Barbecued Spareribs
   ¾ cup prepared barbecue sauce
   ¼ cup finely-chopped onion
   2 teaspoons Worcestershire
      sauce
   1 pound pork spareribs, cut
      into 3-rib pieces
   1 teaspoon salt
   1 cup water

Corn on the Cob
   2 ears corn
   ½ teaspoon salt

Brussel Sprouts
   1 pint Brussels sprouts
   ½ teaspoon salt
   1 tablespoon butter or
      margarine

1. Mix barbecue sauce with onion and Worcestershire sauce.

2. Place rack and water in cooker. Arrange ribs on one side of cooker; pour sauce over ribs. Sprinkle with 1 teaspoon salt.

3. Husk and wash corn. Place ears on square of aluminum foil. Sprinkle with ½ teaspoon salt. Fold up corners of foil to form packet. Place on rack in cooker.

4. Wash Brussels sprouts; trim stems and discard any discolored outer leaves. Place in center of foil square. Sprinkle with ½ teaspoon salt; dot with butter. Fold up corners of foil to form packet. Place in cooker over corn.

5. Cover and set control at 15. Cook over high heat until pressure is reached. Reduce heat; cook 6 minutes.

6. Cool cooker naturally 5 minutes; place cooker under cold, running water to complete pressure reduction.

Makes 2 servings

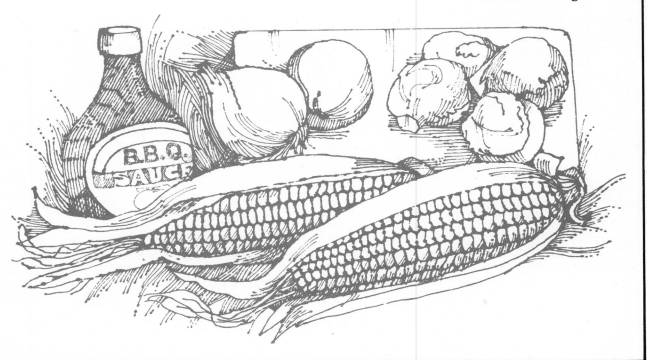

Salmon Dinner

Cook under pressure at 15 lbs. for 5 minutes.

The basic ingredients for this menu can be kept on hand — ready for an evening when you have little time and a hearty appetite. The light, moist salmon loaves go beautifully with an easily-prepared seasoned mayonnaise. You might want to add a tossed salad or assorted crisp, fresh vegetables. The Cherry Crisp can be cooked by itself to complement other menus as well.

Salmon Loaves with Dill Mayonnaise

- 1 can (7¾ ounces) salmon, drained and flaked
- ¼ cup finely-chopped celery
- 2 tablespoons finely-chopped onion
- 2 eggs, separated
- ¼ cup dried bread crumbs
- 1 teaspoon lemon juice
- ⅛ teaspoon salt
- ⅛ teaspoon white pepper
- ⅛ teaspoon dried rosemary leaves
- ¼ cup milk
- 1 cup water
- ¼ cup mayonnaise
- 1 teaspoon prepared mustard
- ½ teaspoon dried dillweed

Parslied Potatoes

- 2 medium potatoes
- ½ teaspoon salt
- 1 tablespoon chopped parsley
- 1 tablespoon butter or margarine, melted

Cherry Crisp

- 1 can (16 ounces) tart cherries
- 1½ teaspoons cornstarch
- ⅓ cup quick cooking oats
- 2 tablespoons light brown sugar
- ⅛ teaspoon salt
- 2 tablespoons sliced almonds, if desired
- 2 tablespoons butter or margarine, melted

1. Mix salmon with celery, onion, egg yolks, bread crumbs, lemon juice, ⅛ teaspoon salt, the pepper and rosemary; stir in milk.

2. Beat egg whites until stiff, but not dry, peaks form; fold into salmon mixture.

3. Divide salmon mixture in half and place each half in the center of an 8-inch square of aluminum foil. Shape foil around salmon mixture to form small loaves, leaving tops open. Place rack and water in cooker. Arrange foil packets on rack.

4. Mix mayonnaise, mustard and dillweed; refrigerate until serving time.

5. Pare and quarter potatoes; place on piece of foil. Sprinkle with ½ teaspoon salt. Combine parsley and 1 tablespoon butter; pour over potatoes. Fold up corners of foil to form packet. Place on rack in cooker.

6. Drain juice from cherries; reserve ½ cup. Combine juice with cornstarch in small saucepan. Cook over medium heat, stirring constantly, until mixture thickens. Remove from heat.

7. Place cherries in small, oven-proof bowl; pour thickened juice over top. Combine oats, sugar, ⅛ teaspoon salt and the almonds; sprinkle over top of cherries. Pour 2 tablespoons butter over oat mixture. Cover tightly with foil. Place on rack in cooker.

8. Cover and set control at 15. Cook over high heat until pressure is reached. Reduce heat; cook 5 minutes.

9. Cool cooker naturally 5 minutes; place cooker under cold, running water to complete pressure reduction.

Makes 2 servings

Tips:

Always check the vent tube by holding the cover up to the light before using pressure cooker; light should be visible through the tube.

Any of the foods in the dinner menu recipes may be prepared separately; use the same amount of water specified for the whole menu. Any foods that require the same cooking time may be prepared together; use the largest amount of water specified for a complete menu. Always reduce heat once pressure has been reached.

Knockwurst Dinner

Cook under pressure at 15 lbs. for 3 minutes.

This is a very quick dinner that's nevertheless special because of the homemade hot potato salad. We like the spiciness of knockwurst, but you can substitute large frankfurters or bratwurst if you wish.

Knockwurst
    1 cup water
    4 knockwurst links

Cabbage
    ½ small head cabbage
    ½ teaspoon salt

German Potato Salad
    3 medium potatoes
    1 medium onion
    ½ teaspoon salt
    4 slices bacon
    1 tablespoon vinegar
    1 teaspoon sugar
    ¼ teaspoon salt

1. Place rack and water in cooker. Arrange knockwurst on rack.

2. Cut cabbage into 1-to 1½-inch wedges; sprinkle with ½ teaspoon salt. Place on rack in cooker.

3. Peel potatoes and onion and cut into thin slices. Place potato and onion slices on 12-inch square of aluminum foil. Sprinkle with ½ teaspoon salt. Fold up corners of foil to form packet. Place in cooker over sausage and cabbage.

4. Cover and set control at 15. Cook over high heat until pressure is reached. Reduce heat; cook 3 minutes.

5. Cool cooker naturally 5 minutes; place cooker under cold, running water to complete pressure reduction.

6. Fry bacon until crisp; drain and crumble. Combine bacon drippings with vinegar, sugar and ¼ teaspoon salt. Pour over potatoes and onions; toss to coat.

Makes 2 servings

Versatile Cooking

Juicy Ham and Yams, Western-Style Barbecued Short Ribs, a colorful Basque-Style Paella and a rich, fruity Steamed Pudding are only a few of the delights featured in the pressure cooker's speedy, convenient repertoire. You can also pressure can a harvest of vegetables, sauces and fruits. And savor the uniquely moist yet crisp fare served up by the new fryers.

Ham and Yams (See recipe on page 40.)

Garden Vegetable Soup (See recipe on page 20.)

Barbecued Short Ribs, Western-Style (See recipe on page 36.)

Basque-Style Paella (See recipe on page 49.)

Trout Amandine (See recipe on page 60.)

Cauliflower with Mustard, Spiced Acorn Squash, Glazed Carrots with Mint
(See recipes on pages 88, 99 and 90.)

Steamed Pudding with Hard Sauce (See recipe on page 117.)

Garden Fresh Vegetable Melange, Fresh Tomato Spaghetti Sauce, Spicy Seckel Pears
(See recipes on pages 151, 150 and 152.)

Scotch Eggs，Fried Chicken (See recipes on pages 148 and 138.)

Pressure Frying

MOST OF THE new low-pressure fryers have been named for one of the foods they cook best—chicken. Wear-Ever calls their fryer the Chicken Bucket; Presto, the ChicknFryer. While it's true, however, that these fryers turn out superb fried chicken, this is by no means the limit of their capability. They do an equally fine job of frying fish, vegetables and many other foods. Indeed, if you haven't tried it before, you'll be amazed by the uniquely crisp, yet moist quality of low-pressure fried foods.

What Is A Low-Pressure Fryer?

A low-pressure fryer differs from other pressure cookers in one significant way: You can use it with vegetable oil instead of water as the cooking medium. All low-pressure fryers are equipped with a weighted pressure regulator that maintains 5 pounds of pressure. Low-pressure fryers can be used with water like standard pressure cookers (although most recipes will take about twice as long to cook as they do at 15 pounds pressure), but *under absolutely no circumstances should a standard pressure cooker ever be used for pressure frying.*

How Do You Use A Low-Pressure Fryer?

Low-pressure frying is not at all difficult, but it requires a careful, attentive cook. First of all, since you're working with hot oil, the danger of a fire or a painful burn always exists. It's a good idea to keep a cookie sheet or jelly roll pan handy whenever you're pressure frying, so that if a fire should break out due to over-heated oil, you can quickly smother it by placing the cookie sheet over the fryer.

Foods that are to be pressure fried should be cut into small, equal-size pieces. To cook a chicken, for example, you should cut apart the thighs and drumsticks, split the breasts, and cut each of the breast halves into two pieces. Vegetables must be cut into uniform pieces.

Always use exactly the amount of food called for in a recipe. If you use less than the specified amount, the food will be overcooked; if you use more, it will be undercooked.

Once the food has been cut into appropriate sizes (the pressure fryer instruction manual will guide you), it must be coated with an egg wash and then coated with a dry flour or crumb mixture. Batter coatings are rarely used because they brown too quickly and tend to disintegrate in the pressure fryer.

For pressure frying, it's essential that the vegetable oil be preheated to a specific temperature, usually 350°F. Once the oil has reached the designated temperature (you will need an accurate deep-fat thermometer to determine this), the food should be added carefully but quickly with tongs or a slotted spoon. Slide the food gently into the oil. Do not drop the food into the oil, for the oil will spatter.

Most foods require a short cooking or browning period in the open fryer; then the cover must be securely closed and the regulator set in place on the vent pipe. Timing begins at this point. This procedure differs from that used for regular pressure cooking: With pressure frying, timing begins the moment the fryer is covered; with pressure cooking, timing begins when the regulator jiggles or rocks to indicate that pressure has been reached.

Once cooking has been completed, pressure must be reduced quickly. To do this, remove the fryer from the heat. Then lift the regulator slightly with the tongs of a long-handled fork and allow the steam to escape. (Never attempt to quick-cool the fryer by placing it under running water!) Once the steam stops rushing out from under the regulator, remove the regulator and uncover the fryer. Using tongs or a slotted spoon, lift the food out of the oil and place it on several layers of absorbent paper to drain.

The recipes that follow have been tested in 6-quart low-pressure fryers. If you have a 4-quart pressure fryer, use your instruction manual as a guide for the correct amount of vegetable oil and food and exact frying and cooking times needed; it may be necessary to make some modifications in our recipes.

Fried Chicken

Cook 5 minutes in open fryer; pressure fry 12 minutes.

Crisp and golden outside and deliciously moist inside, this fried chicken is better than any we've ever bought by the bucketful or fried conventionally. You can reuse the oil for a second batch; allow it to cool, then reheat it to prevent overheating.

½ cup beer or milk
1 egg, beaten
1 cup all-purpose flour
2 teaspoons seasoned salt
1 teaspoon poultry seasoning
1 tablespoon parsley flakes
½ teaspoon pepper
1½ pound chicken, cut into serving pieces
6 cups vegetable oil

1. Combine beer and egg.

2. Combine flour, salt, poultry seasoning, parsley and pepper.

3. Dip chicken into beer mixture; coat chicken completely with flour mixture. Shake off excess flour.

4. Pour oil into 6-quart low-pressure fryer (do not use regular pressure cooker). Heat oil to 350°F over medium-high heat.

5. Using slotted spoon or tongs, carefully place chicken in oil. Cook 5 minutes in open pressure fryer. Stir gently.

6. Cover fryer tightly and place pressure regulator on vent pipe; reduce heat. Pressure fry 12 minutes, adjusting heat so that regulator jiggles gently.

7. Remove fryer from heat. Reduce pressure quickly by lifting regulator gently with tongs of long-handled fork. When steam no longer escapes from under the regulator, remove regulator. Uncover fryer.

8. Using slotted spoon or tongs, remove chicken from fryer and drain on several layers of absorbent paper.

Makes 4 servings

Almond Orange Chicken

Pressure fry 15 minutes.

This fried chicken's crisp coating of flour, almonds and spices does not require browning before it's cooked under pressure. Use ginger ale instead of milk, if you wish, to accent the orange and allspice.

½ cup milk or ginger ale
1 egg, beaten
½ cup all-purpose flour
½ cup ground almonds
1½ teaspoons grated orange peel
1 teaspoon salt
½ teaspoon ground allspice
1¾ pound chicken, cut into serving pieces
6 cups vegetable oil

1. Combine milk and egg.

2. Combine flour, almonds, orange peel, salt and allspice.

3. Dip chicken into milk mixture; coat chicken completely with flour mixture. Shake off excess flour.

4. Pour oil into 6-quart low-pressure fryer (do not use regular pressure cooker). Heat oil to 350°F over medium-high heat.

Almond Orange Chicken (Continued)

5. Using slotted spoon or tongs, carefully place chicken in oil. Immediately cover pressure fryer tightly and place pressure regulator on vent pipe; reduce heat. Pressure fry 15 minutes, adjusting heat so that regulator jiggles gently.

6. Remove fryer from heat. Reduce pressure quickly by lifting regulator gently with tongs of long-handled fork. When steam no longer escapes from under the regulator, remove regulator. Uncover fryer.

7. Using slotted spoon or tongs, remove chicken from fryer and drain on several layers of absorbent paper.

Makes 4 servings

Chicken Parmesan

Cook 5 minutes in open fryer; pressure fry 12 minutes.

Wine brings out the flavor of the Parmesan cheese and Italian seasoning in this fragrant variation of crisp fried chicken.

½ cup dry white, red or rose wine, or milk
1 egg, beaten
¾ cup all-purpose flour
3 tablespoons grated Parmesan cheese
1½ teaspoons Italian seasoning
1½ teaspoons salt
½ teaspoon pepper
1¼ to 1¾ pound chicken, cut into serving pieces
6 cups vegetable oil

1. Combine wine and egg.

2. Combine flour, cheese, Italian seasoning, salt and pepper.

3. Dip chicken into wine mixture; coat chicken completely with flour mixture. Shake off excess.

4. Pour oil into 6-quart low-pressure fryer *(do not use regular pressure cooker)*. Heat oil to 350°F over medium-high heat.

5. Using slotted spoon or tongs, carefully place chicken in oil. Cook 5 minutes in open pressure fryer. Stir gently.

6. Cover fryer tightly and place pressure regulator on vent pipe; reduce heat. Pressure fry 12 minutes, adjusting heat so that regulator jiggles gently.

7. Remove fryer from heat. Reduce pressure quickly by lifting regulator gently with tongs of long-handled fork. When steam no longer escapes from under the regulator, remove regulator. Uncover fryer.

8. Using slotted spoon or tongs, remove chicken from fryer and drain on several layers of absorbent paper.

Makes 4 servings

Curried Shrimp

Cook 5 minutes in open fryer; pressure fry 4 minutes.

Serve these piquant and irresistible shrimp as an hors d'oeuvre or a dinner entrée. Beer enhances the blend of spices and produces a more exciting flavor than milk.

½ cup beer, tomato juice or milk
1 egg, beaten
1 cup all-purpose flour
1½ teaspoons garlic salt
1 teaspoon curry powder
½ teaspoon ground pepper
1 pound fresh or thawed frozen cleaned and deveined shrimp
6 cups vegetable oil
Shrimp cocktail sauce, if desired

1. Combine beer and egg.

2. Combine flour, garlic salt, curry powder and pepper.

3. Dip shrimp into beer mixture; coat shrimp completely with flour mixture. Shake off excess flour.

4. Pour oil into 6-quart low-pressure fryer *(do not use regular pressure cooker).* Heat oil to 350°F over medium-high heat.

5. Using slotted spoon, carefully place shrimp in oil. Cook 5 minutes in open pressure fryer. Stir gently.

6. Cover fryer tightly and place pressure regulator on vent pipe; reduce heat. Pressure fry 4 minutes, adjusting heat so that regulator jiggles gently.

7. Remove fryer from heat. Reduce pressure quickly by lifting regulator gently with tongs of long-handled fork. When steam no longer escapes from under the regulator, remove regulator. Uncover fryer.

8. Using slotted spoon, remove shrimp from fryer and drain on several layers of absorbent paper.

9. Serve with cocktail sauce, if desired.

Makes 4 servings

Tips:
Always turn down heat as soon as pressure fryer cover is in place.
When pressure frying, always fill cooker with vegetable oil as directed by manufacturer; oil may be filtered, covered and stored in refrigerator for repeated use.
Never attempt to deep fry foods in oil in a regular pressure cooker.

Tuna Croquettes with Cheese Sauce

Cook 1 minute in open fryer; pressure fry 2 minutes.

If tuna is one of your favorite foods, you'll especially like the way pressure frying concentrates the flavor in these crisp croquettes.

2 cans (6½ ounces each) water-pack tuna, well-drained and flaked
½ can (10¾-ounce size) condensed cream of mushroom soup
1 cup finely-crushed saltine cracker crumbs
1 egg
2 teaspoons parsley flakes
½ teaspoon celery salt
¼ teaspoon pepper
½ cup milk
1 egg, beaten
6 cups vegetable oil
Cheese Sauce (recipe follows)

1. Thoroughly mix together drained tuna, soup, ½ cup cracker crumbs, 1 egg, parsley flakes, celery salt and pepper. Cover and chill completely, about 2 hours in refrigerator or 20 to 30 minutes in freezer. Shape into balls, using ¼ cup of the mixture for each.

2. Combine milk and beaten egg.

3. Dip tuna croquettes into milk mixture; roll croquettes in remaining ½ cup cracker crumbs, coating completely.

4. Pour oil into 6-quart low-pressure fryer *(do not use regular pressure cooker)*. Heat oil to 350°F over medium-high heat.

5. Using slotted spoon, carefully place croquettes in oil. Cook 1 minute in open pressure fryer. Stir gently.

6. Cover fryer tightly and place pressure regulator on vent pipe; reduce heat. Pressure fry 2 minutes, adjusting heat so that regulator jiggles gently.

7. Remove fryer from heat. Reduce pressure quickly by lifting regulator gently with tongs of long-handled fork. When steam no longer escapes from under the regulator, remove regulator. Uncover fryer.

8. Using slotted spoon, remove croquettes from fryer and drain on several layers of absorbent paper.

9. Serve hot with Cheese Sauce (recipe follows).

Makes 4 servings

Cheese Sauce

½ can (10¾-ounce size) condensed cream of mushroom soup
½ cup (2 ounces) shredded Cheddar cheese
2 tablespoons water
1 teaspoon lemon juice
½ teaspoon parsley flakes

1. Combine all ingredients in small saucepan.

2. Cook over medium heat, stirring constantly, until cheese melts.

Makes 1 cup

Sweet and Sour Pork Chops

Cook 3 minutes in open fryer; pressure fry 12 minutes.

Marinate the chops before frying them and turn the marinade into an Oriental-style pineapple-green pepper sauce — the combination of crisp pork and fruity topping is truly unbeatable!

1 can (6½ ounces) pineapple
  chunks in syrup
  Water (see Preparation)
½ cup cider vinegar
3 tablespoons brown sugar
2 tablespoons soy sauce
½ teaspoon ground ginger
¼ teaspoon ground pepper
6 center cut pork chops, cut ½-
  inch thick (about 1¾
  pounds)
½ cup milk
1 egg, beaten
½ cup fine dry bread crumbs
6 cups vegetable oil
1 green pepper, coarsely
  chopped

1. Drain pineapple, reserving syrup. Add enough water to syrup to make ½ cup liquid. Combine syrup-water mixture with vinegar, brown sugar, soy sauce, ginger and ground pepper.

2. Arrange pork chops in shallow dish. Pour syrup mixture over pork chops. Cover and refrigerate 1 to 2 hours; turn chops occasionally.

3. Remove chops from syrup mixture. Pour syrup into saucepan; set aside.

4. Combine milk and egg.

5. Dip chops into milk mixture; coat chops completely with bread crumbs.

6. Pour oil into 6-quart low-pressure fryer (do not use regular pressure cooker). Heat oil to 350°F over medium-high heat.

7. Using slotted spoon or tongs, carefully place chops in oil. Cook 3 minutes in open pressure fryer.

8. Cover fryer tightly and place pressure regulator on vent pipe; reduce heat. Pressure fry 12 minutes, adjusting heat so that regulator jiggles gently.

9. Meanwhile, add pineapple chunks and green pepper to syrup mixture in saucepan. Cook over medium heat, stirring constantly, until mixture boils and thickens. Reduce heat and keep warm.

10. Remove fryer from heat. Reduce pressure quickly by lifting regulator gently with tongs of long-handled fork. When steam no longer escapes from under the regulator, remove regulator. Uncover fryer.

11. Using slotted spoon or tongs, remove chops from fryer and drain on several layers of absorbent paper.

12. Serve chops with pineapple-green pepper sauce.
Makes 3 to 6 servings

Tips:
Never attempt to deep fry foods in oil in a regular pressure cooker.
Always turn down heat as soon as pressure fryer cover is in place.

Crispy Fried Fish with Tartar Sauce

Cook 3 minutes in open fryer; pressure fry 3 minutes.

Hot, savory crisp-fried fish is one of the great conveniences offered by low-pressure fryers. You'll want to serve this economical and nutritious fare often. You can use fresh fillets, but avoid very thin pieces as these will overcook.

1 pound frozen ocean perch or haddock fillets, thawed (4 or 5 fillets)
½ cup milk
1 egg, beaten
¾ cup all-purpose flour (½ cup cornmeal may be substituted for ½ cup of the flour, if desired)
1½ teaspoons salt
1 teaspoon tarragon, dillweed or other herb
½ teaspoon dry mustard
¼ teaspoon onion powder
¼ teaspoon ground pepper
6 cups vegetable oil

1. Cut each fillet in half crosswise or into pieces approximately 2 x 3-inches.
2. Combine milk and egg.
3. Combine flour, salt, tarragon, mustard, onion powder and pepper.
4. Dip fish into milk mixture; coat fish completely with flour mixture. Shake off excess flour.
5. Pour oil into 6-quart low-pressure fryer (*do not use regular pressure cooker*). Heat oil to 350°F over medium-high heat.
6. Using slotted spoon, carefully place fish in oil. Cook 3 minutes in open pressure fryer.
7. Cover fryer tightly and place pressure regulator on vent pipe; reduce heat. Pressure fry 3 minutes, adjusting heat so that regulator jiggles gently.
8. Remove fryer from heat. Reduce pressure quickly by lifting regulator gently with tongs of long-handled fork. When steam no longer escapes from under the regulator, remove regulator. Uncover fryer.
9. Using slotted spoon, remove fish from fryer and drain on several layers of absorbent paper.
10. Serve with Tartar Sauce (recipe follows).
Makes 4 servings

Tartar Sauce

¾ cup mayonnaise
2 tablespoons sweet pickle relish
2 teaspoons lemon juice
1 teaspoon onion salt
½ teaspoon parsley flakes
¼ teaspoon dry mustard

1. Blend together all ingredients.

Makes ¾ cup

Tip:
When pressure frying, always fill cooker with vegetable oil as directed by manufacturer; oil may be filtered, covered and stored in refrigerator for repeated use.

143

Cocktail Meat Balls

Pressure fry 4 minutes.

These party meatballs will disappear at serving time almost as quickly as they can be fried. They are perfect either as an impromptu appetizer or for a large gathering.

1 pound lean ground beef
¾ cup fine dry bread crumbs
¼ cup pizza sauce or catsup
1 tablespoon instant minced
    onion
1 teaspoon salt
½ teaspoon oregano
½ teaspoon pepper
¼ teaspoon basil or marjoram
½ cup beer, wine or milk
1 egg, beaten
¼ cup grated Parmesan cheese
6 cups vegetable oil
    Pizza sauce, heated,
      if desired

1. Mix together beef, ¼ cup each bread crumbs and pizza sauce, onion, salt, oregano, pepper and basil. Shape into balls, using rounded teaspoons of mixture.

2. Combine beer and egg.

3. Combine remaining ½ cup bread crumbs and cheese.

4. Dip meat balls into beer mixture; roll meat balls in bread crumbs, coating completely.

5. Pour oil into 6-quart low-pressure fryer *(do not use regular pressure cooker)*. Heat oil to 350°F over medium-high heat.

6. Using slotted spoon, carefully place meat balls in oil. Immediately cover pressure fryer tightly and place pressure regulator on vent pipe; reduce heat. Pressure fry 4 minutes, adjusting heat so that regulator jiggles gently.

7. Remove fryer from heat. Reduce pressure quickly by lifting regulator gently with tongs of long-handled fork. When steam no longer escapes from under the regulator, remove regulator. Uncover fryer.

8. Using slotted spoon, remove meat balls from fryer and drain on several layers of absorbent paper.

9. Serve hot with pizza sauce, if desired.

Makes about 3 dozen

Onion Rings

Cook 2 minutes in open fryer; pressure fry 4 minutes.

These onion rings are deliciously delicate — lightly coated with flour and herbs but not smothered by too much breading.

½ pound onions, peeled (2
    medium)
½ cup milk
1 egg, beaten
1 cup all-purpose flour
2 teaspoons salt
1 teaspoon marjoram, if
    desired
¼ teaspoon thyme, if desired
¼ teaspoon ground pepper
6 cups vegetable oil

1. Cut onions evenly into ¼-inch slices; separate into rings.

2. Combine milk and egg.

3. Combine flour, salt, marjoram, thyme and pepper.

4. Dip onion rings into milk mixture; coat onion rings completely with flour mixture. Shake off excess.

5. Pour oil into 6-quart low-pressure fryer *(do not use regular pressure cooker)*. Heat oil to 350°F over medium-high heat.

Onion Rings (Continued)

6. Using slotted spoon or tongs, carefully place onion rings in oil. Cook 2 minutes in open pressure fryer. Stir gently.

7. Cover fryer tightly and place pressure regulator on vent pipe; reduce heat. Pressure fry 4 minutes, adjusting heat so that regulator jiggles gently.

8. Remove fryer from heat. Reduce pressure quickly by lifting regulator gently with tongs of long-handled fork. When steam no longer escapes from under the regulator, remove regulator. Uncover fryer.

9. Using slotted spoon or tongs, remove onion rings from fryer and drain on several layers of absorbent paper.

Makes 4 servings

Fried Mushrooms

Cook 1 minute in open fryer; pressure fry 2 minutes.

Because of the moisture content of mushrooms, they're coated with bread crumbs rather than flour for crisp frying.

½ **pound fresh whole mushrooms**
½ **cup beer or milk**
1 **egg, beaten**
½ **cup seasoned bread crumbs**
1 **teaspoon salt**
1 **teaspoon paprika**
½ **teaspoon ground pepper**
6 **cups vegetable oil**

1. Clean mushrooms by wiping with a damp paper towel or cloth. Trim ends off stems.

2. Combine beer and egg.

3. Combine bread crumbs, salt, paprika and pepper.

4. Dip mushrooms into beer mixture; coat mushrooms completely with bread crumbs.

5. Pour oil into 6-quart low-pressure fryer *(do not use regular pressure cooker)*. Heat oil to 350°F over medium-high heat.

6. Using slotted spoon or tongs, carefully place mushrooms in oil. Cook 1 minute in open pressure fryer. Stir gently.

7. Cover fryer tightly and place pressure regulator on vent pipe; reduce heat. Pressure fry 2 minutes, adjusting heat so that regulator jiggles gently.

8. Remove fryer from heat. Reduce pressure quickly by lifting regulator gently with tongs of long-handled fork. When steam no longer escapes from under the regulator, remove regulator. Uncover fryer.

9. Using slotted spoon, remove mushrooms from fryer and drain on several layers of absorbent paper.

Makes 4 servings

Fried Zucchini

Cook 2 minutes in open fryer; pressure fry 2 minutes.

When zucchini are in season, try them fried for a nutritious snack or a marvelous side dish.

1 pound zucchini (3 to 4 medium)
½ cup milk
1 egg, beaten
½ cup all-purpose flour
¼ cup grated Parmesan cheese
1 teaspoon celery salt
1 teaspoon dry mustard
½ teaspoon marjoram
¼ teaspoon ground pepper
6 cups vegetable oil

1. Cut ends off zucchini; cut crosswise into 1-inch slices.

2. Combine milk and egg.

3. Combine flour, cheese, celery salt, mustard, marjoram and pepper.

4. Dip zucchini pieces into milk mixture; coat zucchini completely with flour mixture. Shake off excess.

5. Pour oil into 6-quart low-pressure fryer *(do not use regular pressure cooker).* Heat oil to 350°F over medium-high heat.

6. Using slotted spoon, carefully place zucchini in oil. Cook 2 minutes in open pressure fryer. Stir gently.

7. Cover fryer tightly and place pressure regulator on vent pipe; reduce heat. Pressure fry 2 minutes, adjusting heat so that regulator jiggles gently.

8. Remove fryer from heat. Reduce pressure quickly by lifting regulator gently with tongs of long-handled fork. When steam no longer escapes from under the regulator, remove regulator. Uncover fryer.

9. Using slotted spoon, remove zucchini from fryer and drain on several layers of absorbent paper.
Makes 4 servings

Cauliflower and Carrots

Cook 3 minutes in open fryer; pressure fry 3 minutes.

This colorful mix demonstrates the unusually flavorful results you'll get by pressure frying vegetables. And because the cauliflower and carrots cook fast, vitamins are retained.

½ pound fresh cauliflower
½ pound carrots
½ cup milk
1 egg, beaten
¾ cup all-purpose flour
2 teaspoons salt
1 teaspoon nutmeg
¼ teaspoon pepper
6 cups vegetable oil

1. Separate cauliflower into flowerets; cut large ones in half. Wash and/or pare carrots; cut into 1-inch slices.

2. Combine milk and egg.

3. Combine flour, salt, nutmeg and pepper.

4. Dip flowerets and carrot pieces into milk mixture; coat vegetables completely with flour mixture. Shake off excess flour.

5. Pour oil into 6-quart low-pressure fryer *(do not use regular pressure cooker).* Heat oil to 350°F over medium-high heat.

Cauliflower and Carrots (Continued)

6. Using slotted spoon or tongs, carefully place vegetables in oil. Cook 3 minutes in open fryer. Stir gently.

7. Cover fryer cooker tightly and place pressure regulator on vent pipe; reduce heat. Pressure fry 3 minutes, adjusting heat so that regulator jiggles gently.

8. Remove fryer from heat. Reduce pressure quickly by lifting regulator gently with tongs of long-handled fork. When steam no longer escapes from under the regulator, remove regulator. Uncover fryer.

9. Using slotted spoon or tongs, remove vegetables from fryer and drain on several layers of paper.

Makes 4 to 6 servings

Cottage Fries

Cook 5 minutes in open fryer; pressure fry 4 minutes.

These crisp potato slices are so good that you won't be able to stop after just one batch. And they cook fast enough to replace frozen french fries.

1 pound potatoes (3 medium), peeled
½ cup milk
1 egg, beaten
1 cup all-purpose flour
2 tablespoons grated Parmesan cheese, if desired
1 tablespoon parsley flakes
1 teaspoon salt
¼ teaspoon pepper
6 cups vegetable oil

1. Cut potatoes into ⅛-inch thick slices.

2. Combine milk and egg.

3. Combine flour, cheese, parsley flakes, salt and pepper.

4. Dip potato slices into milk mixture; coat slices completely with flour mixture. Shake off excess.

5. Pour oil into 6-quart low-pressure fryer *(do not use regular pressure cooker)*. Heat oil to 350°F over medium-high heat.

6. Using slotted spoon or tongs, carefully place potato slices in oil. Cook 5 minutes in open pressure fryer. Stir gently.

7. Cover fryer tightly and place pressure regulator on vent pipe; reduce heat. Pressure fry 4 minutes, adjusting heat so that regulator jiggles gently.

8. Remove fryer from heat. Reduce pressure quickly by lifting regulator gently with tongs of long-handled fork. When steam no longer escapes from under the regulator, remove regulator. Uncover fryer.

9. Using slotted spoon or tongs, remove potato slices from fryer and drain on several layers of absorbent paper.

Makes 4 servings

Scotch Eggs

Pressure fry 8 minutes.

These sausage-jacketed eggs make a great snack with icy glasses of beer or a quick and filling lunch. They're often served with mustard for added tang.

¾ pound bulk pork sausage
6 shelled hard-cooked eggs
1 egg, beaten
½ cup fine dry bread crumbs
6 cups vegetable oil

1. Wrap 1 ounce (2 tablespoons) sausage around each hard-cooked egg. Dip each egg into beaten egg; roll eggs in bread crumbs, coating completely.

2. Pour oil into 6-quart low-pressure fryer *(do not use regular pressure cooker)*. Heat oil to 350°F over medium-high heat.

3. Using slotted spoon, carefully place eggs in oil. Immediately cover pressure fryer tightly and place pressure regulator on vent pipe; reduce heat. Pressure fry 8 minutes, adjusting heat so that regulator jiggles gently.

4. Remove fryer from heat. Reduce pressure quickly by lifting regulator gently with tongs of long-handled fork. When steam no longer escapes from under the regulator, remove regulator. Uncover.

5. Using slotted spoon, remove eggs from fryer and drain on several layers of absorbent paper.

Makes 6 servings

Banana Buckwheat Fritters

Cook 1 minute in open fryer; pressure fry 1 minute.

Enjoy these fresh fruit fritters for dessert or for a special breakfast treat.

4 medium-sized, ripe but firm (green tipped) bananas (about 1½ lbs.)
½ cup ginger ale or milk
1 egg, beaten
½ cup dry buckwheat pancake mix
1 teaspoon cinnamon
½ teaspoon nutmeg
6 cups vegetable oil
Confectioners' sugar, if desired

1. Cut each banana into three equal pieces.

2. Combine ginger ale and egg.

3. Combine pancake mix, cinnamon and nutmeg.

4. Dip banana pieces into ginger ale mixture; roll in pancake mix; coat completely. Shake off excess.

5. Pour oil in 6-quart low-pressure fryer *(do not use regular pressure cooker)*. Heat oil to 350°F over medium-high heat.

6. Using slotted spoon or tongs, carefully place bananas in oil. Cook 1 minute in open pressure fryer. Stir gently. Cover fryer tightly and place pressure regulator on vent pipe; reduce heat. Pressure fry 1 minute.

7. Remove fryer from heat. Reduce pressure quickly by lifting regulator gently with tongs of long-handled fork. When steam no longer escapes from under the regulator, remove regulator. Uncover.

8. Using slotted spoon or tongs, remove bananas from fryer and drain on layers of absorbent paper. Roll in confectioners' sugar.

Makes 2 dozen

Pressure Canning

IF YOU HAVE a pressure cooker that can be used, according to manufacturer's directions, for canning, then you can enjoy the satisfaction and economy of preserving meats, fruits and vegetables in our tantalizing recipes.

Using the pressure cooker to can the Applesauce and Spicy Seckel Pears in this chapter will save time and effort, although it is possible to can fruits without pressure. Pressure canning is the only safe way, however, to can the Garden Fresh Vegetable Melange, Cabbage Soup, Tomato Sauce and Fresh Tomato Spaghetti Sauce. According to the United States Department of Agriculture, meat and vegetable mixtures like these must be cooked in the pressure of steam under pressure (at least 10 pounds) to be sure that they are heated to 240°F — the temperature at which bacteria such as botulism are destroyed.

Some foods must be cooked under pressure for long periods of time — well over an hour — to ensure safety. And, in addition to this initial processing, home-canned meats, vegetables, fish and poultry should be boiled 10 to 15 minutes before you taste or serve them. Because all this cooking does little to enhance plain meats and vegetables, we prefer to freeze these. We use pressure canning for soups, sauces and vegetable blends that actually become more flavorful with prolonged cooking. For basic information on canning plain foods, consult the instruction manual that comes with your pressure cooker. Or write for additional information to the U.S. Department of Agriculture, Washington, D.C. 20402.

Jars For Home Canning

For home canning, only standard glass jars especially made for canning should be used. Do not under any circumstances use ordinary jars such as peanut butter, mayonnaise or other commercial food containers for canning. These jars are not made to withstand the high temperatures necessary for proper processing. Nor are they likely to seal properly.

Use half-pint, pint or quart jars for canning, depending on the kind of food you are canning and the size of your pressure cooker. The instruction manual that comes with your cooker will tell you specific capacity. Though some manufacturers do produce half-gallon mason jars, they generally are not recommended for canning.

Ten Or 15 Pounds Of Pressure?

There seems to be some difference of opinion among pressure cooker manufacturers as to which pressure level to use for canning. Most agree that ten pounds is best. However, at least one leading manufacturer (Presto) recommends canning at 15 pounds pressure and equips its units with nonvariable 15 pound regulators (although you can obtain a variable 5, 10 and 15 pound regulator by writing to Presto at the address given in our Test Reports). The best guideline to follow is your own instruction manual: Read and follow the manufacturer's directions carefully and precisely.

One of the most common problems in home canning is losing liquid from inside jars during processing. This is almost always due to improper canning techniques. Here are the most common causes and ways to prevent them:

• Jars packed too full. Be certain to leave the recommended head space (1/2 inch for all foods except meats, beans and corn, all of which require 1 inch).

• Air trapped in jars. Release excess air bubbles by running blade of knife down side of each jar before closing jars.

• Pressure fluctuations during processing. Heat should be set low enough so that regulator jiggles or rocks gently or dial on gauge remains constant.

• Pressure reduction hastened after processing. Pressure must be allowed to reduce naturally — even though this may take up to an hour for a large, full cooker. Do not try to hurry it by quick-cooling the cooker with water, cold towels or drafts or by nudging or lifting the pressure regulator.

Tomato Sauce

Cook under pressure at 10 lbs. for 15 minutes.

Preserve the tomato harvest to enjoy year round in this fragrant sauce.

2 medium onions, finely
  chopped
3 cloves garlic, minced
3 tablespoons olive or
  vegetable oil
6 pounds tomatoes, peeled,
  seeded, chopped
1 piece orange rind (about 1-
  inch)
2 teaspoons dried thyme leaves
1½ teaspoons dried basil
1 teaspoon salt
¼ teaspoon pepper
2 tablespoons minced parsley
⅛ teaspoon saffron

1. Sauté onions and garlic in oil in large saucepan until tender, about 5 minutes. Add tomatoes and heat to boiling. Cook over medium heat, uncovered, 20 minutes. Purée in blender or food processor.

2. Return tomato mixture to saucepan. Add remaining ingredients. Cook over medium heat until sauce is thickened, about 1 hour.

3. Ladle sauce into prepared jars, leaving ½-inch headspace. Wipe rims and adjust lids.

4. Place rack in cooker. Add amount of water recommended by manufacturer for your cooker. Place jars on rack in cooker, filling as recommended by manufacturer.

5. Cover cooker and set control at 10. Cook over high heat until pressure is reached. Reduce heat; cook 15 minutes.

6. Remove cooker from heat and reduce pressure naturally. Uncover cooker; remove jars and place on cooling rack or folded cloth.

Makes 3 pints or 6 half pints

Fresh Tomato Spaghetti Sauce

Simmer sauce 60 minutes. Cook under pressure at 10 lbs. for 75 minutes.

You don't have to choose between the convenience of purchased spaghetti sauce and the incomparable flavor of homemade when you have this rich blend in your pantry.

2 tablespoons vegetable oil
2 medium onions, chopped
2 carrots, pared, chopped
2 cloves garlic, minced
1 pound ground beef
1 pound mild Italian sausage
10 medium tomatoes (about 3
  pounds) peeled, seeded
2 cans (8 ounces each) tomato
  sauce
¾ cup dry red wine or beef
  broth
¼ cup snipped parsley
1 tablespoon dried basil
1 teaspoon sugar
1 to 1½ teaspoons salt
¼ teaspoon ground nutmeg
¼ teaspoon ground black
  pepper

1. Heat oil in Dutch oven. Sauté onions, carrots and garlic in oil until tender, about 5 minutes. Stir in beef and sausage. Cook over medium heat until meat is no longer pink. Stir in remaining ingredients. Heat to boiling; reduce heat and simmer uncovered until thick, stirring occasionally, 1 hour.

2. Ladle sauce into hot jars, leaving 1-inch headspace. Wipe rims and adjust lids.

3. Place rack in cooker. Add amount of water recommended by manufacturer for your cooker. Place jars on rack in cooker, filling as recommended by manufacturer.

4. Cover cooker and set control at 10. Cook over high heat until pressure is reached. Reduce heat; cook 75 minutes.

5. Remove cooker from heat and reduce pressure naturally. Uncover cooker; remove jars and place on cooling rack or folded cloth.

Makes about 5 pints or 10 half-pints

Garden Fresh Vegetable Melange

Cook under pressure at 10 lbs. for 40 minutes. (See recipe how-to on page 80.)

The colors of this zucchini melange are as tempting as the aromas of the basil, oregano, garlic and onion that spice it.

2 pounds unpeeled zucchini (about 6 medium), cut into ⅛-inch slices
2 medium onions, chopped
1 large green pepper, cut into strips
1 large clove garlic, minced
3 tablespoons vegetable oil
2 pounds tomatoes, peeled, cored, cut into chunks
1 teaspoon salt
1 teaspoon dried basil leaves
1 teaspoon dried oregano leaves
1 teaspoon sugar
¼ teaspoon pepper
2 cups water

1. Sauté zucchini, onions, green pepper and garlic in oil in kettle or Dutch oven about 5 minutes. Stir in remaining ingredients. Heat to boiling. Boil 2 to 3 minutes.

2. Ladle vegetable mixture into prepared jars. Cover with boiling vegetable liquid, leaving ½-inch headspace. Wipe rims and adjust lids.

3. Place rack in cooker. Add amount of water recommended by manufacturer for your cooker. Place jars on rack in cooker, filling as recommended by manufacturer.

4. Cover cooker and set control at 10. Cook over high heat until pressure is reached. Reduce heat; cook 40 minutes.

5. Remove cooker from heat and reduce pressure naturally.

6. Uncover cooker; remove jars and place on cooling rack or folded cloth. *Makes 4 pints*

Cabbage Soup

Simmer soup 10 minutes. Cook under pressure at 10 lbs. for 45 minutes.

This hearty soup harmonizes the flavor of cabbage with those of pears, tomatoes and dill. Top each steaming bowlful with a dollop of sour cream for a delicious accent.

2 medium onions, chopped
¼ cup butter or margarine
4 cups thinly-sliced cabbage (about ¾ pound)
2 pears, pared, chopped
2 pounds tomatoes, peeled, quartered, excess seeds removed
1½ tablespoons fresh dill or 2 teaspoons dried dillweed
2 teaspoons sugar
½ teaspoon salt
⅛ teaspoon pepper
2 cups beef broth
1½ cups water

1. Sauté onions in butter in kettle or Dutch oven until tender, 4 to 5 minutes. Stir in cabbage and pears. Cook and stir 2 to 3 minutes longer or until cabbage is slightly limp. Stir in remaining ingredients. Heat to boiling. Reduce heat and simmer 10 minutes.

2. Ladle soup into prepared jars, leaving ½-inch headspace. Wipe rims and adjust lids.

3. Place rack on cooker. Add amount of water recommended by manufacturer for your cooker. Place jars on rack in cooker, filling as recommended by manufacturer.

4. Cover cooker and set control at 10. Cook over high heat until pressure is reached. Reduce heat; cook 45 minutes.

5. Remove cooker from heat and reduce pressure naturally.

6. Uncover cooker; remove jars and place on cooling rack or folded cloth. *Makes 4 pints*

Spicy Seckel Pears

Cook under pressure at 5 lbs. for 10 minutes.

The beautiful golden color and spicy aroma of this preserve recommend it as a food gift as well as a pleasing dessert. Only about two-inches wide, small Seckel pears are perfect for canning whole. If they're not available, you can use pared larger pears, cut in half, with stems and cores removed.

6 pounds firm-ripe Seckel pears
2 cups cider vinegar
6 cups sugar
3 cinnamon sticks, each about 2-inches long
1½ tablespoons whole cloves
1 teaspoon whole allspice

1. Cut peel from pears, leaving stems intact and pears whole. Combine remaining ingredients in large saucepan. Heat to boiling. Boil 5 minutes.

2. Pack pears into prepared jars. Pour in hot syrup leaving ½-inch headspace. Wipe rims and adjust lids.

3. Place rack on cooker. Add amount of water recommended by manufacturer for your cooker. Place jars on rack in cooker, filling as recommended by manufacturer.

4. Cover cooker and set control at 5. Cook over high heat until pressure is reached. Reduce heat; cook 10 minutes.

5. Remove cooker from heat and reduce pressure naturally.

6. Uncover cooker; remove jars and place on cooling rack or folded cloth.   *Makes 6 pints or 3 quarts*

Applesauce

Simmer apples 25 minutes. Cook under pressure at 5 lbs. for 15 minutes.

This old-time favorite can be made with almost any kind of apples, but the fruit will vary in sweetness and texture. It may be necessary to add more water to the sauce if apples seem dry or more sugar if the sauce seems bland.

3 pounds apples, pared, cored, cut into eighths
2 tablespoons lemon juice
1 stick cinnamon, about 2 inches long
¾ cup sugar

1. Place apples, lemon juice, and cinnamon stick in kettle or Dutch oven; cover. Simmer until apples are tender, about 25 minutes. Remove cinnamon stick. Stir in sugar. Purée or leave chunky.

2. Ladle sauce into prepared jars, leaving ½-inch headspace. Wipe rims and adjust lids.

3. Place rack in cooker. Add amount of water recommended by manufacturer for your cooker. Place jars on rack in cooker, filling as recommended by manufacturer.

4. Cover cooker and set control at 5. Cook over high heat until pressure is reached. Reduce heat; cook 15 minutes.

5. Remove cooker from heat and reduce pressure naturally.

6. Uncover cooker; remove jars and place on cooling rack or folded cloth.   *Makes 5 half-pints*

Test Reports

THE FOLLOWING pressure cookers were evaluated according to quality and ease of performance. Careful attention was paid to the clarity and comprehensiveness of the instruction manual provided with each cooker. All testing was done on a gas range and each cooker was tested with water only, prior to recipe testing, to insure that it would reach pressure and operate properly. Once we determined that the cookers functioned correctly, we tested a variety of recipes from the appropriate instruction manual provided with each unit as well as a single beef entrée recipe as a constant standard for all. In all cases, the recipes in the manuals yielded foods that were overcooked to our taste. Most manufacturers recommend that you use their recipes only as guidelines; we certainly agree. In those cookers designated by the manufacturers as suitable for canning, we canned two types of vegetables according to the canning procedures presented in the manuals.

It should also be noted that virtually all the pressure cooker models tested also come in other sizes. We have found a 4- or 6- quart size most convenient for everyday use and small-scale canning, but if you plan to do much canning, you may prefer a larger size. The larger cookers can also be used for everyday meal preparation, but you should use additional liquid, as specified by the manufacturer.

In testing low pressure fryers, we followed procedures similar to those used with other pressure cookers. Since the pressure fryers are designed for cooking with either oil or water at 5 pounds pressure, we supplemented the tests with deep frying recipes. We omitted the canning tests, since canning cannot be accomplished in the fryers. We cannot overemphasize the importance of carefully reading and following the directions provided by manufacturers for low pressure frying to avoid the damage of burns caused by hot oil. Nor can we overstress the fact that low pressure frying in oil should *never* be attempted in other pressure cookers.

All-American #907

This 7-quart (liquid capacity) pressure cooker looks like a piece of institutional cooking equipment. Actually, it is a small version of the professional canner/cookers manufactured by this company. Made of polished heavy cast aluminum, the cooker weighs about 9 pounds. Its design is significantly different from the other cookers we tested, featuring a manually-operated control valve that sits on a vent pipe and opens to vent air from inside the cooker and closes to contain it. If an overpressure condition should ever exist within the cooker, the valve is set to automatically "pop off" at 20 pounds pressure. The valve can be removed for cleaning. An easy-to-read steam gauge is located prominently atop the cooker. It is calibrated to register internal pressure between 0 and 20 pounds. Past 20 pounds, the gauge is clearly marked "caution."

The main difference between this cooker and others we tested is in the sealing system. All the other brands we tested used a rubber ring/gasket to seal the cooker's cover to the body. With the All-American, the seal is metal to metal (no rubber ring is used). Both the cover and body are precision machined to interlock snuggly. Four sturdy plastic knobs screw tightly on the top to clamp the cover to the body, ensuring an airtight seal. If overpressure conditions occur, though, the metal-to-metal seal will automatically vent steam to prevent an explosion.

Additional features of this cooker include an automatic excess pressure release and a sturdy plastic handle to lift the cover. Arrows marked on the cover and body clearly mark the correct closed position. According to the 65-page instruction manual, a cooking rack is included with the cooker, though one did not accompany the unit we tested.

We liked working with the All-American in our tests, but were not very impressed with the instruction manual. The cooker was easy to use and reached pressure quickly. It was relatively easy to maintain desired pressure without much readjusting of the gas burner. We particularly liked the pressure gauge: It's nice to know exactly what the pressure is inside the cooker, instead of having to wait for the regulator to rock or jiggle as you must with other brands.

The cooker was especially nice for canning. Not only are you able to see what the pressure is (and thereby control it better), but you also have the flexibility to can at 5, 10 or 15 pounds pressure. In our tests both carrots and green beans canned at 10 pounds pressure turned out very nicely.

We did note some disadvantages to this cooker. First, we spotted a steam leakage around the cover. Since it always occurred at the same location, we think the cover was warped slightly. We also found that the cover closure knobs got too hot to handle. The same goes for the aluminum side handles used for carrying the cooker. It would be easy to burn yourself if you forgot to use pot holders.

From a safety standpoint, the most important disadvantage of this cooker is that it does not have a mechanism to lock the cover in place when there is pressure inside, which means that you could open the cooker under pressure. We didn't try!

We didn't like the instruction manual provided. We found it disorganized, not as comprehensive as it could be, and dated. In correspondence received from the manufacturer, we were told that the company has been making pressure cookers since the 1930s and the design in basically the same now as then. Our guess is that the same is true for the instruction manual. It's just not in step with the lifestyles and tastes of the majority of Americans today. Directions are provided, for example, on what time of the day to slaughter an animal and how to cool the carcass!

In spite of its disadvantages, we still think this cooker is worth considering as a purchase. It's sturdy, durable, has been proven over the years and is comfortable to work with, once you understand pressure cooking. Its biggest selling point, though, is the adjustable pressure capability that makes it versatile for both cooking and canning.

Approx. Retail Price: $39.95

MacDonald's #M1010

This company manufacturers pressure cookers designed for home canning and quantity cooking. The unit supplied to us for testing was a 10-quart model.

The cooker is very sturdy and functional looking. It's made of aluminum with a burnished cast finish and is heavy, weighing about 9 pounds. It has a calibrated steam gauge similar to the one found on the All-American #907. The gauge will register internal pressure between zero and 20 pounds. The cooker also has a pressure regulator weight that's designed to jiggle and release steam when pressure reaches 15 pounds inside the cooker.

Near the center of the cooker is a small rubber over-pressure valve with a metal center stem. This stem functions in the same manner as the air vent/cover lock on the Presto units: it raises when there is pressure inside the cooker and lowers when there is none. Thus, it acts as a visual indicator of pressure. Other features of the #M1010 include a rubber gasket that fits into a groove in the cover and forms a seal when the cover is locked in place, wooden handles on the lid and body of cooker, clearly marked "open" and "closed" positions, a

metal trivet for canning and steaming, and a 29-page instruction manual.

We're sorry to report that this cooker failed completely in our tests. We tried numerous times to get it to work but couldn't. We never even had a chance to try cooking or canning with it, because we were never able to get it to reach pressure. A close inspection revealed a serious defect in the construction of the lid. Apparently when the aluminum was die-cast, it was molded in such a way as to prevent a seal from forming. We contacted the manufacturer several times to tell them of this problem and to request another unit for testing. One was never provided; therefore, we cannot recommend the MacDonald's #M1010.

Approx. Retail Price: $20.90

Mirro-Matic Deluxe (#M-0594)

This 4-quart top-of-the-range model is made of aluminum and is particularly nice for pressure cooking because it's equipped with an automatic 3-way pressure control that can be set for 5, 10 or 15 pounds of pressure. The unbreakable one-piece control sits on top of the vent pipe and regulates the amount of pressure in the cooker. When there is pressure inside the cooker, the control jiggles to provide what the manufacturer calls "cooking without looking" (meaning you can always hear it cooking at pressure).

Other features of the Mirro include a self-sealing rubber gasket that seals the cover to the body, plus three safety devices: a safety fuse that will release if water in the cooker is depleted or if the cooker overheats and builds up too much pressure; a lock lever in the handle that locks into position when there is pressure in the unit and prevents the cooker from being opened; a lift pin assembly that moves the lock lever into or out of the locked position when pressure increases or decreases inside the cooker. Contoured plastic handles located on both the body and cover make the cooker easy to open and close. An aluminum cooking rack rounds out the features of this cooker, which carries a UL-Listing and Good Housekeeping Seal as well as a limited one-year warranty.

The Mirro Deluxe was easy to use and always reached pressure quickly. In several of our tests, however, we had difficulty maintaining the directed "1 to 4 jiggles per minute," which is supposed to indicate that the correct level of pressure is being maintained. Either the control jiggled vigorously or not at all, even with repeated attempts at adjusting the gas flame under the cooker.

A domed cover to accommodate glass canning jars makes this cooker especially suitable for canning, though its small 4-quart size is somewhat limiting. Our canning attempts were successful, though we had trouble maintaining the required 4 jiggles per minute. We had to keep readjusting the gas flame under the cooker to try to maintain a constant pressure. This could cause a potential problem when canning because fluctuations in pressure may cause liquid to be drawn from the jars, although this did not happen in our tests.

Mirro's 65-page instruction manual is quite comprehensive. It includes illustrated step-by-step usage directions; recipes, directions and/or timetables for preparing beef, pork, lamb, veal, poultry, game, fish, seafood, vegetables, soups, pasta, and desserts; information on adapting other recipes to pressure cooking; high altitude cooking directions; information on sterilizing baby bottles and surgical instruments; and a comprehensive canning section. Several pages of questions and answers cover just about everything you might be uncertain about.

Approx. Retail Price: $26.95

Mirro-Matic Standard (#M0536)

This Mirro is a 6-quart top-of-the-range aluminum model. Unlike the Mirro Deluxe model we tested, this one can be used for cooking at 15 pounds of pressure only because it has a standard one-way regulator. For this reason, the manufacturer does not recommend this model for canning.

Other than a different pressure regulator, this Mirro has the same features as the #M-0594: a self-sealing rubber gasket inside the cover; a safety fuse that will release if an overpressure situation develops inside the cooker; a lock lever in the handle to prevent the cooker from being opened under pressure; a lift pin assembly that locks and unlocks the lever; contoured, easy-to-hold plastic handles; clearly marked open/close positions on the cover; an aluminum cooking rack; a limited one-year warranty; and UL-Listing plus the Good Housekeeping Seal.

Like the other Mirro, this one is uncomplicated to use and always reached pressure quickly and with no difficulty in our tests. As with the other Mirro, though, we had some difficulty maintaining the "1 to 4 jiggles per minute" that the manufacturer recommends. With some foods we had no problem; with others, we got either vigorous jiggling or none at all, even with repeated adjustments of the gas flame under the cooker.

The manual provided with this model is similar to and as comprehensive as the other one from Mirro, containing everything but the canning section and the medical equipment sterilization information. If you are buying a pressure cooker with an eye toward canning in it, this one would not be an appropriate choice. However, if you have no interest in canning and plan to use a cooker for pressure cooking only, you will not be disappointed with this unit.

Approx. Retail Price: $31.95

Presto #01/PS4

This is a 4-quart stainless steel cooker designed to cook a variety of foods under pressure. It's very basic — with no gimmicks. It has a removable standard regulator, which sits atop the vent pipe and maintains a constant 15 pounds of pressure within the cooker. According to the manufacturer, this is the ideal cooking and canning pressure. In addition to automatically exhausting air from inside the cooker, the air vent/cover lock acts as a visual indicator of pressure in the cooker (when it's in the raised position, there is pressure inside).

To prevent the cooker from being opened when under pressure, a special locking bracket on the inside of the unit engages with the air vent/cover lock when it is raised. As an added safety feature, an overpressure plug is located under the cover handle to automatically release steam if the vent pipe clogs and steam cannot be released normally. A sealing ring that fits inside the cover forms a pressure-tight seal between cover and body of the cooker. "Open" and "close" positions are marked on the cover; a cooking rack is provided and the unit is UL-Listed and carries a limited 1-year warranty.

This pressure cooker performed well in our tests. It was easy to work with, reached and maintained pressure as the 69-page instruction manual said it would and posed no operational problems. We were very impressed with the instruction manual. It's thorough, easy to understand and well organized and includes sections on operating, cleaning and servicing the cooker and high altitude conversions. There is one problem with this instruction booklet, however, that could be considered a major drawback. The booklet has been written to cover at least four different Presto models. In spite of the fact that at the beginning of the booklet the instructions advise that 15 pounds of pressure is "ideal for cooking and canning," only the conscientious reader will note in the fine print of the 10-page canning section at the back that the manufacturer says: "Do not can in the PS4 Model Stainless Steel Pressure Cooker." Including canning information in an instruction manual for a pressure cooker model that should not be used for canning could be dangerous!

Approx. Retail Price: $41.90

If, despite the manufacturer's directive that all foods benefit from being cooked at 15 pounds pressure, you wish to use any of the Presto cookers at 5 or 10 pounds pressure, you can obtain a 3-piece, variable weight pressure regulator by writing to the Home Economics Department of National Presto Industries, Eau Claire, Wisconsin 54701. This replacement regulator will fit any of the current models of Presto cookers and canners, including the electric pressure cookers.

Presto #01/PA6H

This top-of-the-range pressure cooker is a basic model designed for cooking and canning. Its features are identical to those on the Presto #01/PS4: a standard 15 pound pressure regulator, vent pipe, air vent/cover lock, locking bracket under the cover handle, removable sealing ring, overpressure plug and cooking rack. But the PA6H is a 6-quart cooker made of aluminum with a painted (Harvest Gold) finish. (The PS4 is a 4-quart stainless steel model.)

This cooker was easy to use and performed well in all our cooking and canning tests with one exception: In one test we had some difficulty maintaining a slow rocking motion of the regulator — either the regulator rocked vigorously or it didn't move at all. This was, however, exceptional; we didn't have any trouble on other tests.

In addition to cooking with this model, we canned green beans and carrots. The first canning test was not too successful — a substantial amount of the liquid in the jars was drawn from the containers. The problem was not with the cooker but with our technique; we learned that you must regulate the heat under the pressure cooker carefully. In the initial 5 minute exhausting period (where air inside the cooker is vented out) we had the burner set too high, which caused a rapid venting of steam and probably drew the liquid from the jars.

Our second canning attempt was much more successful. No liquid was lost from the jars, processing went smoothly and a gentle rocking of the regulator was easy to maintain. The food looked and tasted good and was firm textured. We would rate this cooker as acceptable for canning (vegetables, at least), even though there is some controversy about whether canning can be done at 15 pounds pressure. Our testing showed that it can, providing manufacturer's instruction are followed exactly. (If you wish to obtain a variable pressure regulator for Presto cooker, see test report on Presto Model #01/PS4.)

The 69-page instruction manual that comes with this cooker is the same one that accompanies the Presto PS4 model. The PA6H is UL-Listed and carries a limited one-year warranty.

Approx. Retail Price: $35.90

Presto GranCookerie Whole Meal Maker (#01/PE6)

With this model, Presto has turned the pressure cooker into an electric appliance. Cooking is still done under pressure, but heat is regulated by a detachable control (just like those on electric fry pans) instead of a stove burner. Virtually the same foods can be prepared in the GranCookerie as with a conventional top-of-the-range pressure cooker and the unit may be used for canning.

The body of the 6-quart GranCookerie is finished inside and out with a special Presto nonstick coating that is easy to clean as well as good looking. The cover on the cooker is aluminum with a durable painted finish and is well marked with open and close positions. Plastic handles located on each side are easy to grasp and don't get hot when unit is heated. The heat control regulates temperature with calibrated settings from Warm to 400°F.

Other features of the GranCookerie are the same as for other Presto pressure cookers: a standard 15 pound pressure regulator (with a variable regulator available; see test report on Presto model #01/PS4), vent pipe, air vent/cover lock, locking bracket under the cover handle, removable sealing ring, overpressure plug and cooking rack. The unit is UL-Listed and has a limited one-year warranty. Presto calls their GranCookerie the "Family-Size Whole Meal Maker." It is a whole meal maker (you can prepare entree, vegetable and desserts at the same time) but whether it's family-sized depends on the size of your family. The appliance can accommodate meals for one to four persons at one time. We tried canning fresh carrots and green beans in the GranCookerie and were pleased with the results. When following Presto's directions exactly, we had no problems. Processing went smoothly, little or no liquid escaped from the jars and the food looked and tasted good. Overall we were quite pleased with the GranCookerie. But we did run into a couple of problems worthy of consideration. Throughout our testing we noticed a slight steam leakage under the cover. Though it did not seem to pose any safety threat, any steam leakage from a pressure cooker is undesirable and potentially hazardous. We also found that the nonstick finish scratched easily. The outside of the cooker scratched after just a couple hand washings with other dishes; the inside scratched when a long-handled fork was used to turn over browning meat and poultry. Aside from questioning most of the cooking times provided, we liked Presto's 69-page instruction manual. As usual, Presto is thorough about explaining operation, maintenance and servicing of the appliance.

Approx. Retail Price: $69.90

Presto WeeCookerie Whole Meal Maker (#01/PE3)

The WeeCookerie is a small version of the GranCookerie. It has a 3-quart capacity, is electric with a detachable heat control and has all of the same features the GranCookerie has (see test report on Presto GranCookerie). Since it is half the size of the GranCookerie, it cooks half as much food at one time. The only real difference between the two, apart from size, is that Presto does not recommend canning in the WeeCookerie.

The WeeCookerie will cook whole meals for one person or small portions for two, as well as most foods that can be done in top-of-the-range models.

Test Reports

As with the GranCookerie, the WeeCookerie performed well in our tests. It was easy to use, reached and maintained pressure with no apparent problems and cooked food that was acceptable. The WeeCookerie's instruction manual is basically the same as that provided with the GranCookerie.

The WeeCookerie is UL-Listed and has a limited one-year warranty.

Approx. Retail Price: $59.90

SEB Aluminum Super Cooker

Imported from France, this top-of-the-range cooker is designed to pressure cook and can. It's made of heavy gauge aluminum and has a liquid capacity of 4.5 liters (about 4 1/2 quarts).

Features of the cooker include a pressure regulator (though the manufacturer doesn't call it that, but rather a "rotating valve") that maintains 8 pounds of pressure in the unit; a vent pipe to release steam from inside; a safety valve that will automatically release if an overpressure condition occurs; a stainless steel clamp that fits across the cover and under two side brackets; a rubber sealing ring to seal the cover to the body; insulated plastic side handles; and a collapsible vegetable basket.

We put this cooker through its paces on cooking and canning tests and have mixed feelings about recommending it. It performed reasonably well in testing. It always reached and maintained pressure without difficulty. The seal was tight and no steam leakage was spotted anywhere. Most foods, including canned carrots and beans, were acceptable.

The main reason we hesitate to recommend this pressure cooker is because it may be used only for cooking at 8 pounds pressure. You wouldn't know that, though, from reading the accompanying 249-page cookbook instruction manual. Nowhere is this information given — we had to call the manufacturer's distributor to get it. Because the SEB is a low pressure cooker, you will have difficulty using recipes with it from any source other than the cookbook provided. And that spells trouble, especially because the SEB cookbook/instruction manual is not very good. Clearly, this cookbook/instruction manual has simply been translated from French to English with no regard for the differences between French and American kitchen equipment and ingredients. Information is provided on how to assemble and operate the cooker, but it is sketchy. Virtually no general pressure cooking information is offered. As mentioned, SEB doesn't even tell you at what pressure you're cooking. The manufacturer claims this is "the only cooker that can be opened under pressure while cooking." In fact, it can be opened but that's because it does not have a safety locking mechanism. We really don't think this is an advantage as the manufacturer would try to lead you to believe. Any pressure cooker can be opened, if desired, during the cooking process simply by cooling

shortly under cool water to reduce pressure and unlocking the safety lock.

Other minor complaints included "insulated" plastic handles that were too hot to touch when the cooker was heated and cleaning instructions that tell you *not* to clean the cooker's cover with soapy water. A small detachable foil sticker on the clamp advises us that the cooker is UL-Listed, but no mention of this is made on the package labeling or in the instruction manual.

Approx. Retail Price: $37.95

SEB Stainless Steel Super Cooker

This 4.5 liter, stainless steel top-of-the-range pressure cooker is a twin sister to the SEB aluminum model. The only difference between them is the metal used; other features are exactly the same (see SEB Aluminum report for complete listing and discussion). *Approx. Retail Price: $56.95*

Low Pressure Fryers
Wear-Ever Chicken Bucket (#90026)

Despite its name, this 6-quart top-of-the-range low pressure fryer is designed to speed fry many foods besides chicken and to cook a variety of foods under pressure. Major features of the unit include a pressure regulator that snaps onto a vent tube and controls the pressure within the cooker at 5 to 6 pounds; four safety vents located in the cover to release excess pressure if vent tube clogs or cooker overheats; oil level lines marked inside to indicate correct amount of oil for pressure frying; and a rubber gasket inside the cover edge to seal the cover to the body when the cooker is closed and pressure is reached. Additional features include a heavy-duty clamp which fits across the top of the cooker and under two side brackets when cover is in place. A knob with a ballpoint locking screw tightens the clamp. Handles are situated on the sides of the cooker to permit lifting and carrying. Also available in a 4-quart size, the unit is UL-Listed.

We found that the Chicken Bucket performed very well in tests for both pressure frying and pressure cooking. Chicken, when prepared with an egg/milk wash and a coating of seasoned flour then fried as directed, was delicious and done just right. In our tests for pressure cooking, the Chicken Bucket was quite successful.

Assembling and operating the Chicken Bucket seems confusing at first: You have to turn the knob that tightens the clamp first clockwise, then counterclockwise. Once you get the hang of it, however, it's easy. The first time we used the unit, we couldn't get the pressure regulator to rock as directed. Since we didn't have that problem again, we assume it was because of something we did wrong, not any fault of the cooker. On a green bean test, we had a lot of steam leakage and the cooker wouldn't reach pressure. The problem was our fault. We didn't completely dry the gasket, as directed, before assembling.

We found that it is necessary to watch the pressure regulator rather closely. The rocking action is very slight and the cooker is quiet so you must watch closely to determine when pressure is reached or your timing may be off (this applies only to pressure cooking, not frying, which is timed from when the cooker is closed). The only other thing we noticed was that occasionally during frying under pressure, some loud bubbling oil noises could be heard; apparently, these were not significant.

Since the Chicken Bucket is not equipped with a mechanism to lock the cover in place when there is pressure inside the cooker, it is possible to open the unit when it's under pressure. We tried it once — as expected, the steam rushed out.

The 35-page instruction manual includes step-by-step illustrated sections on how to pressure fry and cook. It features a good but small collection of recipes for various fried foods, charts for frying vegetables and fish, plus hints on how to improve frying technique and correct any possible mistakes. For pressure cooking, it covers various foods with charts on how to prepare the food, amount of water to use and time to cook. Information on ordering replacement parts and a brief question/answer section fill out the manual.

Approx. Retail Price: $34.95

Wear-Ever Electric Chicken Bucket (#72026)

This model is the same as the Wear-Ever #90026 except that it operates electrically. It's an aluminum 6-quart low pressure fryer with a removable black plastic base that encloses the heating element and protects the counter or table top. Like the #90026, this unit can be used for low pressure frying, deep fat frying or low pressure cooking. A detachable heat control probe with ten settings regulates frying and cooking temperatures. Other features on this fryer match the #90026; a five pound pressure regulator that sits on a vent tube; four safety vents in the cover; oil level lines; a rubber sealing gasket; a cover clamp fitted with a locking screw; side brackets to hold the clamp; handles for lifting. The unit is UL-listed.

The Electric Chicken Bucket produces some fine eating. We used it to fry a variety of foods, including chicken, fish, onion rings, potatoes and other vegetables. We had no problems operating the unit and it consistently worked well. The only exception to its fine performance showed up on a pressure cooking test for round steak: The meat burned onto the bottom of the pot, even though we had the heat control set at a very low setting, as directed. Apparently, this tends to happen with this unit, because the instruction manual specifies that a cooking rack (none

is provided) may be used when preparing meats.

Since this model is identical in design to the #90026 (see test report), the comments we had about the confusing assembly of the cover and clamp arrangement apply here, too. As with the #90026, it would be possible to open this model when it's under pressure since there is no automatic cover locking mechanism. However, the manufacturer makes the user aware of this potential danger.

The 67-page instruction manual is similar to the one accompanying the nonelectric Wear-Ever Chicken Bucket. The recipes are the same except for time/temperature adjustments. Included in the manual are step-by-step illustrated sections on how to pressure fry and cook, safety precautions, charts for frying and cooking a variety of items and information on ordering replacement parts.

The decision on whether to buy this appliance should be based on two factors: Will it get enough use to justify purchase and is it worth the rather high price tag to you?

Approx. Retail Price: $59.95

Presto ChickNFryer (#01/PF6)

Presto has entered the pressure fryer market with this 6-quart top-of-the-range model. The ChickN-Fryer boasts many features similar to other Presto pressure cookers: The regulator sits on a vent pipe that releases excess pressure from the cooker, but the regulator maintains 5 pounds of pressure inside the cooker instead of 15. An air vent/cover lock on the cover automatically exhausts air from inside and acts as a visual indicator of pressure. A locking bracket on the inside of the cooker engages with the air vent/cover lock to prevent the cover from being opened when the unit is at pressure. A sealing ring inside the cover forms a tight seal between the cover and the body of the unit when there is pressure inside. An overpressure plug under the handle automatically releases steam if the vent pipe clogs.

A nonstick finish covers the outside and inside of the cooker body. An oil level line on the inside indicates the correct amount of oil to be used for pressure frying. Plastic handles, which require pot holders when the unit is heated, are located on the sides. Close and open positions are clearly marked on the cover. Also available in a 4-quart size, the ChickN-Fryer is UL-Listed and has a limited one-year warranty.

We followed the Presto instructions precisely on all of our tests and the ChickNFryer performed well. In our pressure cooking tests, the ChickNFryer performed well, too. As usual, Presto has done a nice job with their 39-page instruction manual. They include complete information on operation, maintenance and part replacement/servicing of the ChickNFryer, directions for pressure frying and cooking and a limited assortment of basic recipes.

Approx. Retail Price: $47.90

Index

Index